The Love Triangle Murderer

Anna Benjamin

Published by Trellis Publishing, 2021.

While every precaution has been taken in the preparation of this book, the publisher assumes no responsibility for errors or omissions, or for damages resulting from the use of the information contained herein.

THE LOVE TRIANGLE MURDERER

First edition. July 2, 2021.

Copyright © 2021 Anna Benjamin.

ISBN: 979-8224859245

Written by Anna Benjamin.

THE LOVE TRIANGLE MURDERER

ANNA BENJAMIN

1

Some female killers simply don't want to get their hands dirty and to the deed themselves. Instead, they ask someone else to murder for them. It might seem impossible, but these things truly do happen more often than we think. These women would either hire a person who is not personally involved or a lover who can be easily manipulated to help. The motivation can be self-preservation, especially if a woman is in an abusive marriage and wants to run away. But some women do kill for financial gain. This is exactly what happened to Andie Gasper who was caught in a deadly love triangle. His wife Cheryl had a long-term affair with Randall Knight who was madly in love with her. She manipulated him with her lies in order for him to kill her husband so they could collect his life insurance money.

The case shook the small town of Yorkshire to the core because the residents were not used to this level of violence. Andie was shot and murdered in a very public place, and even though the investigators did identify the killer almost right away, Randall managed to slip through the fingers of justice. The Gasper family was losing hope once the case turned cold. But the investigators were resilient and determined to find new leads that would prove that Cheryl Gasper was behind everything. They worked day and night for years to see what went wrong in the first trial and make Randall speak to them openly about the incident. And sixteen years later, they finally uncovered the truth.

Early life

Cheryl Gasper was born on September 8th, 1962. She was a gorgeous young woman who would draw attention wherever she appeared. Cheryl had many suitors when she was in her late teens and early twenties, but only one man was interesting enough for her to consider getting married to him. His name was Andie Gasper, and he was the same age as Cheryl. Andie was ambitious and wanted to make something of his life, but he also needed the support from the people who were closest to him. He didn't want to live the rest of his life in a small town. Cheryl and Andie got married, and he decided to pursue military carrier which was very common back in the day. This meant that his new family would have to move around the United States with him and Cheryl agreed to do so.

They relocated to Carswell Air Force Base in Fort Worth, Texas and soon the kids were on the way. Cheryl gave birth three times during the 1980s, and the situation in the Gasper family seemed to go smoothly. Andie helped out whenever he could and he was feeling very happy with the fact that the family was growing. Cheryl was still looking gorgeous, and she took a good care of herself. She was known as one of the most beautiful military wives in the base, and she enjoyed to be seen that way. What Andie didn't know was that his wife started an affair with a fellow Air Force soldier named Randall Knight. He lived nearby, and the two would meet occasionally. Randall and Cheryl managed to hide their relationship throughout the entire decade, sneaking around. Of course, it continued after both men were discharged from the army because Randall was truly in love with Cheryl.

Randall moved to Cuyahoga Falls, Ohio while the Gaspers bought a house in Cattaraugus County, New York. Randall and Cheryl remained in contact, talking to each other over the phone and meeting in motel rooms every now and then. The lovers were not able to see each other as often as they wanted, but Randall really wanted to make it work. They also constantly wrote letters to each other, exchanging them on a weekly basis. Randall was deeply in love with Cheryl, and he was certain that their relationship had a future even though he was only her lover. But he had no idea that Cheryl slept with several people beside him. She was very attractive and in her early thirties which made her especially appealing to other men. But Cheryl knew how to keep a secret and make Randall feel like he is the only one.

Cheryl was getting bored with her family life, but she didn't want to divorce her husband. She started talking to Randall, making up horrible details about her family life, hinting that Andie was abusing her. She slowly started adding more information and dropping hints which made Randall particularly emotional. He wanted to help her as much as he could and be her prince in shining armor. But as 1993 rolled in, the romance was becoming weaker and Randall and Cheryl started growing apart. He refused to kill Cheryl's husband even though she asked openly several times before. The two of them broke up in December of the same year. Cheryl started seeing even more men from the neighborhood, but she kept the letters that were sent to her by Randall.

One afternoon, Andie's mother Melanie was cleaning their family house when she discovered one of the envelopes. She was curious about the contents, so she opened it and read the text. She was shocked to discover that it was sent to Cheryl because the sender went into details, describing different sexual encounters he had with her. Andie's mother was appalled by Cheryl's behavior, and she went straight to her son with the evidence that his wife was cheating on him. It looked like Andie never suspected anything during the years he was married to her because he quickly packed up his bags and left the family home. Cheryl became reckless, and that led to her family breaking up. However, she saw it as a good thing because she was free to do whatever she wanted now. On the other hand, her finances were running low, and the divorce would drain her bank account. Cheryl needed to come up with a new plan, and she remembered Randall who was willing to do anything she asked of him.

The day of the murder

It was July 3rd, 1994 and the day was very warm just like every summer in Yorkshire, Cattaraugus County, New York. Cheryl Gasper contacted her on and off lover Randall Knight on July 2nd and began her standard story of the abuse she was suffering from her husband Andie. She asked him to drive over from Ohio so they could meet. Randall told her he would think about it. Cheryl really needed a man at that time and since she wasn't sure if Randall would actually accept her invitation, she called another friend of her husband. Randall did decide to drive to New York State from Ohio to see Cheryl, but he was unpleasantly surprised when he arrived at her house. There was a man inside and Cheryl was making love to him. Randall saw everything as he was standing outside the bedroom window.

Completely disappointed and heartbroken because he thought that he was Cheryl's only lover, Randall made a decision to call Andie and do what Cheryl asked of him. Perhaps it was his own way of trying to get back with her, or he felt the anger that needed to be released somewhere. Andie did find out about Randall and Cheryl a couple of months before, but the two men never had a conversation about it. Andie probably presumed that Randall wanted to apologize to him since he hinted that they needed to discuss something important. The two agreed to meet at a local shopping plaza that afternoon.

Randall Knight listened to Cheryl's accounts of the relationship she had with Andie, and he was certain that her husband was physically abusing her. Since they did discuss the possibility of removing Andie from the picture, collecting the insurance money, and purchasing a dream house together, Randall thought that plan might still work. He would save Cheryl and kickstart their love life by killing Andie. Once they saw each other in the parking lot, Randall approached the man's car and got inside. He immediately confronted him about his violent behavior to his wife, and they started arguing. Andie had no idea what Randall was talking about, and he tried to defend himself. He was startled when Randall lunged at him and stabbed his chest with a knife. The blade went through the seatbelt. Randall quickly ran away from the scene of the crime.

Since the parking lot behind the shopping plaza was frequented by people, the police were called quickly. A passerby noticed something odd behind one of the stores and decided to contact the authorities. A patrol car arrived, and a police officer exited the vehicle, looking around for signs of trouble. He only found one parked car behind the store. Once the police officer approached that vehicle, he noticed that a man was sitting behind a steering wheel. He thought that the man was asleep and tried to wake him up. However, he saw that his shirt was bloody and that the man had a chest wound. Seeing that the wound was fresh, the police officer called the ambulance in hopes of saving the man's life.

The ambulance arrived in minutes, but they determined that the man was dead and they couldn't do anything to help. Other policemen appeared at the crime scene, and the first thing they needed to do is determine who the man was. They ran the car plates through the directory and discovered that his name was Andie K. Gasper. He had a local address. The forensics started working on the car because there was a possibility that the killer left a trace behind. The analysis determined that Andie Gasper was probably surprised by the attack since he was still wearing his seatbelt. This led police to think that it was either a robbery or Andie was attacked by someone he knew.

There were almost no clues that could point a finger at a single individual. The murder weapon was nowhere to be found. The interior of the car was spotless, and they couldn't find any traces of someone else being inside. But Andie's keys were not in the car which was an odd detail. It was clear that the murder will be difficult to solve because the investigators had no leads. But they did go to Andie's place of residence to talk to his wife Cheryl. She was devastated when the officers told her what happened to Andie and everyone believed her at the time. The whole neighborhood was shocked with the news of what happened to Andie. They wanted to help in any way and started thinking about the last time they saw Andie. One neighbor remembered a strange detail that caught his eye just a day before the murder.

The neighbors knew each other really well and could easily spot strangers coming and going. One man saw an unknown vehicle parked in front of Andie Gasper's home which was an unusual sight. Thinking there might be something suspicious behind the visit of this person, the neighbor wrote down the license plates. When he learned about the murder, the same neighbor remembered what he saw, and he told the police the tag number of the car that was parked on their street. After running them through the system, the police discovered that the suspicious car belonged to a man called Randall Knight who was from Ohio. They weren't sure if they had an actual lead but the officers decided to pursue it. Perhaps Randall witnessed something at the Gasper residence that could point in the wife's direction.

The police quickly discovered that Randall Knight knew the Gasper family well and that they considered him to be an old friend. They met while the Gaspers were living in an Air Force base in Texas and remained close. However, the detectives weren't ready to discover how close Knight's bonds really were with the Gasper family. After all, he was Cheryl's lover for years.

The investigation

The police started interviewing Andie Gasper's family, including his parents. They told the investigators that he was currently separated from his wife Cheryl and that Andie was living with them. Andie's mother discovered a letter written by Randall Knight that revealed the affair the two had. Andie was heartbroken and disappointed but he did have three kids with Cheryl, and it was impossible for him to walk away completely. He was also unsure about the divorce and Andie was stalling with the process, trying to find the best solution. Andie visited Cheryl and the kids often. He was back at his old family house on the day of the murder, mowing the lawns. This confirmed the suspicions that Randall Knight was involved in the killing. However, there was no way they could link Cheryl to it.

Cheryl had a prepared alibi for the day of the murder, and she told the investigators that she was at a barbeque. Her friends confirmed the story and she did, in fact, spend an afternoon with them. When asked about Randall Knight, she admitted that she knew him and that they have been involved, but she was unaware if he actually did murder her husband. She seemed honest during the interview, and the detectives thought that Randall might have been a jealous lover who wanted to get rid of the competition. There was nothing which could suggest that Cheryl made Randall commit the murder. The authorities couldn't find any physical evidence linking Randall to the scene of the crime, but they had more than enough circumstantial evidence to bring the man in for questioning.

He was back in Ohio and didn't contact Cheryl since the day her husband died. Randall Knight was interviewed in Ohio and then transferred to Cattaraugus County. The detectives who were working on the case decided they might have their main suspect. Randall did admit to being in town when the murder occurred, but he wouldn't provide more details. They did think that Randall was covering for Cheryl at this point because he firmly said she was not involved. He also didn't speak about Cheryl at all and avoided that topic altogether. He remained silent even when he was informed that he would go on trial for the murder of Andie Gasper.

The first trial

Randall Knight was arrested a couple of months after the murder, and he was on a fast track to face the judge in the courtroom of Cattaraugus County Court. His trial started at the beginning of 1995, and numerous witnesses were called to the stand, including Cheryl Gasper herself. Randall pleaded not guilty at the start of the procedure, and he remained calm during the process. Andie Gasper's mother was one of the witnesses since she discovered the letter than connected Randall to Cheryl and she told the jury of the way her son felt after he found out about the affair. Melanie Gasper described Andie's disappointment and the fact that he was considering divorcing Cheryl as well as taking custody of their three children from her.

When Cheryl came up to the stand, she did admit to the affair but told the courtroom she had nothing to do with the murder of her husband. She claimed that Randall did it all by himself without telling her anything in advance. She didn't mention the pressure she put on Randall Knight years before the crime occurred because it would clearly implicate her in the murder. Cheryl omitted the abuse claims she told Randall in private. The trial lasted for months and the jury made their decision – they found Randall Knight not guilty of the murder of Andie Gasper. This news shocked everyone because it meant that the case would remain open since there was no conclusion. The investigators were certain that they got their man and that Cheryl was somehow involved, but they had absolutely no proof to confirm this theory.

The reopening of the cold case

Without any new leads or evidence, the murder of Andie Gasper quickly became a cold case, gathering dust in the local Sheriff's Office. However, Undersheriff William Nichols believed that there was more to be uncovered in this case and he pressed the Cold Case Unit to review the files in hopes of finding something they missed the first time around. William Nichols knew plenty about the murder since he was one of the investigators who worked on the case from the very beginning. He became the main detective in 2002 which gave him permission to put this case on the very top of the priorities.

is when he received a phone call from Andie Gasper's parents, asking him to do something about the killing of their son. They were tired of waiting and needed a resolution because the clock was ticking.

The police knew who did it, but they needed someone who would finally start talking about the events that occurred in Yorkshire in 1994. Nichols was persistent and once they ran out of options, he suggested calling the reinforcements. His idea was to get the FBI interested in the case. It was an excellent move because the FBI had the right people who might help them out.

They worked together on the case up until 2009, hoping they would find something. And they did! The investigators noticed several federal violations that could have been helpful in the first trial. The detectives called the FBI, telling them about what they found in the paperwork and they arranged a meeting with the U.S. Attorney's Office who helped them restart the case. Even though there were no physical evidence or any new DNA, the investigators suspected that Cheryl Gasper broke the federal law by being involved in a murder for hire. The detectives found out that Cheryl talked to Randall about the murder itself back in 1992 and that he even wanted to kill Andie in March of 1994 when he crossed the state lines with the intention to end Andie's life. That was more than enough to finally arrest the woman because she did in a way hire Randall to kill her husband.

But first, the investigators needed to speak with Randall Knight. They arrested him at the beginning of 2010. Since he couldn't be charged with the same crime twice because he was found not guilty in the first trial, the detectives focused on getting the whole story out of him. Randall was willing to talk this time around which was a positive change. He confirmed their suspicions about crossing the state lines. Plus, Randall gave the investigators the missing pieces they needed to build the case against Cheryl Gasper. He told them the following: *"I killed Andie Gasper by stabbing him once in the chest. Cheryl told me she wanted me to kill Andie and she didn't care when or how."*

He revealed that the main goal was Andie's life insurance that was supposed to bring $100,000 to them. Cheryl convinced Randall that they could start their lives over far away from everything and build a dream house for just the two of them. That was everything Randall wanted to hear. However, the money was never paid up because the insurance company determined that Andie's signature on the life insurance policy was fake. Randall didn't want to ask Cheryl about the money because he didn't want to risk involving her in the murder. That is why he shied away from contacting her afterward. Randall managed to score a plea deal for his cooperation and was facing twenty to thirty years in prison which was better than a life sentence.

Cheryl Gasper moved to Chaffee, New York and maintained a low profile for years. However, she was picked up by the police on May 19th, 2010 and transferred to Cattaraugus County where she was facing charges for a second-degree murder of her husband. It seemed like she was expecting to be arrested because Cheryl had gone away with the police willingly. One of the attorneys who prepared the case said the following: *"This charge is the result of the perseverance and dedication of law enforcement officers who refused to give up. While today's charge does not bring Mr. Gaspar back, it will hopefully provide some closure to Mr. Gaspar's family."* Cheryl remained in jail, waiting for a trial that was set to begin in autumn of 2010.

The second trial

Cattaraugus County Court was packed on October 5th, 2010. Numerous friends and family members waited for this trial for sixteen years. Andie's and Cheryl's kids were there as well. And finally, Cheryl Gasper, the woman who plotted to kill her then-husband with her lover entered the room. Once a beautiful and seductive woman looked sullen and sad knowing that she was about to be questioned about the events that occurred back in 1994 and possibly be sent to prison for life. She immediately pleaded guilty in front of Judge Larry M. Himelein who continued to question her for a good part of the next ten minutes.

Cheryl nearly whispered her words while speaking to the judge. Everyone had a hard time hearing what she had to say. Cheryl confirmed her involvement, supporting Randall's claims that the two spoke about the murder years prior to the event. The judge was satisfied with her answers, agreeing to her guilty plea of the second-degree murder. Cheryl wanted to avoid being prosecuted by the FBI so she gave up her right to an appeal. Her defense lawyer read the following message to the journalists gathered in front of the courthouse: *"I regret that my involvement with Randall Knight has caused pain to my children and family. If it were not for their love and support I could have not made it through this ordeal."* She was sent back to prison to wait for the sentencing.

Randall Knight appeared in the courtroom to hear his sentencing on November 3rd, 2010. His lawyer Kimberly Schechter told the judge that her client was used by Cheryl Gasper because she knew how much he loved her and that Randall would do anything for her. The judge did take this into consideration but watching the faces of Andie's parents eagerly waiting for justice for the murder of their son was probably the stronger image. Randall apologized to everyone who was present, and they all stood waiting for the judge's decision. He was sentenced to twenty-four years in federal prison. Andie's parents were relieved. His father Horace later said: *"We knew from day one that they were both involved."*

Cheryl Gasper was back in the courtroom on November 15th, 2010. Both Andie's parents and her own kids were in the room as well. Judge Larry M. Himelein read the sentence that said Cheryl will serve eighteen years to life in a prison. She remained calm as she heard the final decision because that was more or less what she expected. Cheryl turned around to face her family and the in-laws, apologizing to them for causing so much pain. Horace Gasper, Andie's father said the following after the sentencing: *"We watched due process finally happen in the courts. It's been a long time to get to this point."*

The aftermath

Randall Knight was not happy with his defense in the last trial claiming that they did not do a proper job presenting his case in front of a judge. He filed a complaint to the appeal court who reviewed the case and ordered that it should be returned to federal court. Randall also claimed that the statute of limitations had run out for the charge he was sentenced for. He pleaded guilty in 2010 which was eleven years too late for murder-for-hire in New York State. This actually did make a huge difference when the federal court took a second look at the case.

Randall's sentence was reduced by ten years on February 13th, 2015 which left him a total of nine years to spend behind the bars.

SHE MADE THEM KILLERS: THE TRUE STORY OF BARBARA OPEL

14

JESSI NIXON

In 2001, Barbara Opel murdered a 64 year old man – but committed the act by paying a group of five teenagers, including her own 13 year old daughter, to do her dirty work. On April 13, Jerry Duane Heiman was ambushed by the small group, who attacked him with knives and baseball bats to complete the job. Opel's younger children, 7 and 11 years old, followed their mother's instructions to assist the teenagers by mopping up Heiman's blood.

The body was discovered eight days later, in a shallow grave located just ten miles away from the house.

Blind trust

Heiman, who had been diagnosed with terminal cancer, had hired Opel in the fall of 2000 to care for his 89 year old mother, who was afflicted with advanced Alzheimer's disease. A Boeing retiree, Heiman provided Opel and her children with something they'd never experienced before – stability.

The brash, overweight mother and her three young children – Heather, 13, an 11 year old son and a 7 year old daughter – had resided in 22 places in just seven years, including a stint where they lived out of the family car. Welfare authorities reported that Opel had been evicted from 10 different apartment buildings for non-payment of rent.

Heiman should have been a godsend. Opel and her children moved into the basement of his home in Everett, Washington, while he lived upstairs with his mother. However, Opel was more than just ungrateful – she was abrasive. Although she frequently initiated arguments with Heiman, he allowed himself to trust her. She was even permitted to write cheques from his bank account to cover household expenses.

But his faith gave Opel some insight into Heiman's prosperity – and she wanted the $40,000 in his bank account for herself. He'd made the money through the sale of a house, and according to prosecutors, the large sum was enough to give her a motive for Heiman's murder.

Hatching a plan

Described by her own sister as "brain-dead," Opel came up with a murderous plot to eliminate Heiman and take control of his finances – but her plan depended on the help of her bright young daughter, Heather, and her group of friends.

Although she'd been raised into a nomadic kind of lifestyle, Heather was a smart, motivated young woman. Her grades were high, and she excelled as a basketball player. In fact, her biggest dream was to someday star in the WNBA – but in the short term, she was hoping to get a dirt bike.

Just a month before Heiman was killed, an entry in Heather's diary showed how she planned to get the bike of her dreams – "so my mom said if I helped kill Jerry I can go get one."

Heather's friends would also receive rewards for their roles in Opel's scheme – she promised cash payments to anyone Heather could recruit to help carry out the murder. Heather managed to find a female friend, Marriam Diane Oliver, who was also 14. Along with three other adolescent boys, the two girls broke into Heiman's room one night in March 2001 armed with bats and knives, but were too scared at the time to carry out Opel's plan.

But just a month later, Heather had managed to pull together a second hit squad to take out her mother's boss. She'd developed a crush on an older boy named Jeff Grote, who was 17 years old, muscular, and worked at the local skating rink.

Opel recognized this crush as an opportunity to bring the strong young man under her wing, and immediately invited Grote to move into the Heiman house with the family – even promising him a private room where he could have sex with her young daughter. He agreed, and found himself under Opel's influence.

She persuaded Grote to put together a new hit team, including his friend Kyle Boston, 15, and Boston's 13 year old cousin – along with Heather and her friend Marriam. In exchange for his participation in the murder, Opel promised, Grote would receive a car and new clothes.

The Bostons would receive $300 to split between them, and Oliver would be given enough money to purchase new skates. Heather, of course, would finally get her dirt bike.

Unusually close

The relationship between Heather and her mother was not your typical mother-daughter bond. According to Heather, the two were unusually close – more like sisters, or friends, than a mother and daughter.

"I just felt like I could tell her anything," she said. "And she was always there with me whenever I went anywhere."

According to Heather's 79 year old grandmother, who relocated to a motel in Everett to regularly visit her daughter and granddaughter in prison, described Heather's childhood as happy – painting a sweet picture of a caring mother who loved to bake chocolate chip cookies with her eager children, laughing together while making a mess of the kitchen.

However, the defense brought in a clinical psychologist who described Heather as "abnormally" loyal and obedient – the kind of child who would likely be unable to stand up to a dominating, controlling mother. This characterization was reinforced by witnesses, including Heather's baseball and basketball coaches. They described how Opel would scream at Heather from the sidelines during games – often bringing the star athlete and "nice kid" to tears.

"I couldn't believe it," said Lane Erickson, who coached a Boys and Girls Club ball team in Everett. "Heather was the only girl on the boys team, and she was the best player by far. The only problem was that the mom would yell and scream at her, and Heather would start crying."

Another coach testified that Opel's out of control, overbearing attitude was so severe that he assigned her the role of assistant coach in an effort to curb her behaviour from the dugout.

Even Heather's father Bill Opel, who divorced Barbara back in 1990, remembered his daughter as being quiet and withdrawn – and maintained that her only downfall was her unfailing allegiance to her domineering mother.

"There's not a right and a wrong way – the only way Heather knows is mom's way," Bill said. "And Heather does not question mom."

Still, allegations of abuse have followed Opel since Heather was born in September, 1987. Not even a year later, neighbours at the Opels' Mill Creek apartment complex were complaining to authorities that she was screaming at her newborn baby.

"The level of violent screaming is escalating," said one anonymous caller. "Recently, one of the neighbours has heard slaps to the baby."

A visit to the apartment was conducted by Child Protective Services (CPS), but reports indicated that the workers found the baby clean and displaying no evidence of abuse. Still, the calls continued – two years later, CPS received a call from the landlord, who said Opel "has been yelling at Heather since the child was three months old."

The landlord added that worried neighbours had also contacted the police, who reported back that the apartment was clean and the toddler was unbruised and well-fed. But the neighbours kept complaining, even advising CPS that Heather and her siblings were being left unsupervised.

According to a former neighbour, Megan Slaker, the kids were often locked out of the house. She would invite them to help her with yard work, and said she prayed for them regularly.

"She just didn't want them in the house, I guess," she said. "You feel compassion for children who you don't think are getting the love and attention they need. I wanted them to feel some love."

Chris Perry lived across the street from Opel and her children for a couple of years. She said Opel had previously lived next door to her best friend, and she wasn't pleased to see the family relocate to her neighbourhood.

"She was a lady I would never forget in my entire life," Perry said. "She was just so mean – screaming at her kids all the time, all hours of the night. You would never hear her lovingly talking to her children."

Opel and Heather's father Bill each accused each other of mistreatment and abuse, and the couple's divorce was described as "an active battleground" by a psychologist. Opel's second marriage has also been compared to a battleground – and even Heather admitted she had a tough time growing up.

"I have some real scars," she said, noting that she began experimenting with drugs like marijuana and ecstasy when she was only 11 years old. "But I felt like I was really starting to pull through it."

She began drinking then, as well, and particularly enjoyed Bacardi spiced rum.

"I shouldn't have done the drugs, and I shouldn't have hung out with the people I did hang out with," she said.

Although Heather claims her mother was not to blame for her misbehaviour, Opel was not a positive influence on her daughter. In February 2001, she hosted a Valentine's Day party for her kids at Heiman's home – and according to one 12 year old guest, the kids were welcome to drink beer, smoke marijuana, use the hot tub in the backyard, and have sex in Opel's bedroom.

While she said she didn't engage in any of this behaviour, her father was furious to learn about the illicit activities – he'd been assured by Opel that night that the party would be safe.

"I'm absolutely shocked – I'm ashamed I let my daughter spend the night there," he said. "I trusted (Opel)."

By that point, Heather was really starting to clean her life up. Her focus had shifted from drugs and alcohol to basketball and other athletics, and she had started working to get her schoolwork on track. She was determined to achieve her dream of playing in the WNBA.

"I sat down and just started writing all my goals," she explained. "I wrote about 100 of them."

During their messy divorce, Bill engaged Opel in a drawn-out custody battle in an attempt to secure at least the right to visit his children. She refused to stick to the agreed-upon visitation and kept the children from him for years, he said. Court records show that in 1997, prosecutors managed to charge her with custodial interference, but the charge was dropped because they felt a jury wouldn't convict.

Eventually, Bill admitted he just gave up, moving to Wenatchee with his new wife and their children.

"I couldn't chase it anymore," he said. "I've just been writing my child-support checks and hoping they go to a good cause. Guess they didn't."

Carrying out the job

On April 13, Jerry Heiman came home to an ambush. The five teenagers attacked him as soon as he stepped in the door, with one cracking him hard on the head with an aluminum bat. He had no idea who the children were, and he started begging for mercy.

"Who are you?" he cried out. "What do you want?"

While the larger teenager beat him with the big bat, two others hit him repeatedly with souvenir bats from the Seattle Mariners. Finally, the two girls appeared with a 10-inch kitchen knife, which they used in turns to stab him until he was dead.

"He looked me straight in my eyes and begged me to help him," Oliver later explained. "All I could do was drop the knife and run and not get him help either."

Oliver had gotten squeamish, and retreated into the basement where Opel was hiding with her two younger kids. But Opel wouldn't let her quit.

"Get up there and do what you're supposed to do," she hollered at the girl until she complied. "You're supposed to be Heather's friend. You're supposed to be there for her!"

When the job was done, Opel and her murderous team celebrated with a nice dinner and a night at the Rodeway Inn – paid for with

Heiman's credit card. The very next day, Opel used his checkbook again to rent a truck, packing it up with the dead man's valuables. She didn't get far, though.

Heiman's son Greg had traveled from Arkansas to visit his father in the days after Heiman was murdered. After spending three and a half hours wandering around Sea-Tac Airport waiting for his dad to pick him up, Greg eventually took a shuttle to his father's home in Everett. The scene he discovered was horrifying.

The lights were all off, and the doors were locked. The shades were drawn, so Greg couldn't even see inside the seemingly deserted home. Once he climbed in through a side window, he found his grandmother alone in the house – sitting in her wheelchair, her mouth full of shredded pages from a magazine. All of the furniture was gone, save for a couple of lawn chairs, but the hot tub outside was still running. Later, Greg found dried blood spotted on the garbage can and on the chandelier.

He went looking for his father the next day. Within the week, Heiman's body had been found wrapped in sheets and buried in a shallow grave on the Tulalip Indian reservation. In an attempt to prevent authorities from identifying the body, acid had been poured all over it.

It wasn't long before Barbara Opel was brought in for questioning. She and the five teenagers were quickly charged with the murder.

"That was fun!"

According to the district attorney who prosecuted the case, the teenaged killers were "monsters" who displayed "cold indifference" to what they'd done. Prosecutors attested that after stabbing Heiman, Heather Opel exclaimed in delight, "That was fun! I want to do it again!"

But according to an article from the Seattle Post in August 2002, she learned fast that her actions had very serious consequences.

"In my room, I just sit and stare at my bricks. I'm like, 'look what you got yourself into,'" Heather told reporter M.L. Lyke.

At her sentencing, Heather publicly apologized to the Heiman family – and read aloud a poem she wrote in her cell, lamenting the fact that despite all her efforts to be a "good girl," people still seem to think she's "bad."

"People just look at me that way, and I'm just like, why can't they look at the good side of me?" she said.

Defense attorneys argued that, coming from broken families, the young people were vulnerable and easily swayed by the bullying and abusive tactics demonstrated by Barbara Opel. Still, the judge's determination was that the "hands-on nature" of an attack carried out with clubs and knives made the children candidates for adult court – except for Mike Boston, who was just 13 years old.

Heather, who was 13 at the time of the killing, pleaded guilty and received a sentence of 22 years with no possibility of parole.

"Her mother used her as payment for murder, then commanded her to kill, too" said Seattle attorney Michele Shaw, who argued that Heather had been manipulated fost of her life. "She is a victim herself."

Just 14 years old when she was convicted, Heather will be released from prison at the age of 35. She still hopes to play professional basketball upon her release. She also retains the right to appeal the judge's decision to try her as an adult – and if she wins the appeal, she could cut more than ten years off this 22 year prison term.

"She was responsive, compliant, respectful in every way," said her former principal, Jim McNally. "She was always surrounded by friends. This was a devastating blow to us. To see someone with so much potential in such crisis – it's beyond words."

Marriam Oliver, 14, received 22 years, and 14 year old Kyle Boston was sentenced to 18 years. Boston's cousin Mike will be held in a juvenile prison until he is 21 years old. Heather's boyfriend, Jeffrey Grote, also pleaded guilty and received a sentence of 50 years. In a description he wrote to an online pen pal, Grote claims he is an "easygoing, humorous person," and "a big teddy bear."

At her own trial in 2003, Barbara Opel testified that it was the kids who wanted to kill Heiman – she'd only wanted him to be hurt, she stated. Defense attorneys portrayed Heiman as an abusive drunk.

"I guess I thought that if Jerry got beat up bad he deserved it," she said. "The only thing that had been on my mind was everything the kids and I had been through."

Heiman had mistreated her daughter, Opel claimed, and she'd gotten so fed up with his behaviour that she frequently made comments like, "I wish he was dead" to her family and friends. According to Opel's defense attorney Peter Mazzone, she'd simply gotten swept up in an attack that got out of control.

In his argument, Mazzone said Grote was to blame. He wanted to move in with the Opel's, Mazzone told the jury, but Opel said that if he was to do so, he would need a car to help her run errands like taking the younger children to school. She admitted that after Heiman was killed, she used his credit cards to take the teenagers on a shopping spree.

"I had no way to pay for my kids," she testified when Mazzone asked what she was doing with the dead man's credit cards. "No way else to get food."

She claimed she'd been "horrified" by the murder, stating that if she'd known Grote and his friends had intended to kill Heiman, she would have never let him move into the house. However, once the killing had been carried out, she felt it was her responsibility to protect her daughter, who had been involved.

But according to deputy prosecuting attorney Chris Dickinson, this wasn't the first time Opel had tried to have Heiman killed. He told the jury that Opel had attempted at least four previous plots to murder her employer – and finally managed to convince a group of teenagers who grew up in broken homes to carry out her evil scheme.

"She took them in," he explained, "partied with them, gave them a place to hang out."

Convicted and sentenced

As the jury was unable to reach a unanimous decision after seven hours of deliberation, Opel managed to avoid being sentenced to death – keeping her from going down in history as the first woman on Washington's death row. While seven jurors supported the prosecution's case for the death penalty, five others felt life in prison was a more appropriate sentence.

According to juror Sally Toffic, one of the five women who served in the trial, the jury spent hours listening to Opel's confession to police and carefully examined all of the evidence – but there was no convincing those who pushed for a life sentence.

"We wanted to make sure we didn't leave a single stone unturned," she said. "But we just got to a point where there was no reason to continue on."

However, Opel still received a life sentence without the possibility of parole, on the conviction of aggravated first-degree murder. Another 12 months was added for her abandoning Heiman's invalid mother, and five additional months for theft. Opel did admit to the jury that she "hated" abandoning the elderly woman, who ended up passing several days without food or water.

"I didn't want to leave her," said Opel, who had helped feed and care for Heiman's mother. "I wanted her to come along with us."

Opel was also banned from having any contact with her children – but her sentence means that she may eventually serve out her sentence in the same prison as her daughter Heather. Once Heather and Oliver turn 18, they would be relocated to Washington Women's Correctional Center in Purdy – the facility where Opel will spend the rest of her life.

"Your fundamental right of seeing your children is lost when you do to your children what Barbara did to hers," said Superior Court Judge Gerald Knight.

Opel wept as the jury's decision was read, whimpering and wrapping her arms around her defense attorney. According to Mazzone, he and partner Brian Phillips had worried throughout the trial, second-guessing all their witnesses and words as if "someone's life depended on it."

"It's the right result," Mazzone said after the verdict was handed down. "Today is Good Friday, and the theme is life."

In order to return a death sentence, the jury would have needed to reach the unanimous conclusion that there were no mitigating circumstances to spare her life – and defense attorney Brian Phillips presented the court with at least five.

Testimony provided by a neuropsychologist and a neuropsychiatrist suggested Opel suffered from impaired brain function – but Toffic admitted that while some jurors believed the argument, others dismissed it as "psychobabble." In her opinion, none of the potential mitigating circumstances was convincing.

"Everyone had their own reason for voting the way they did," she said. "There were a surprising number of different reasons that people had for their vote."

Alternate juror Christine Wintch admitted after the trial that her vote would have been for the death penalty. Although she heard all the testimony presented in the case, she was not part of the jury's deliberations – and Wintch came to her conclusion after learning Opel could potentially serve the majority of her sentence in the same facility as Heather. In fact, a corrections officer reported that during the trial, Opel commented that she hoped to be reunited with Heather in prison so they could continue to "kick ass" there.

However, Superior Court Judge Gerald Knight's recommendation was that Opel not be housed in the same prison as either Heather or her best friend, Marriam Oliver. Since their sentences were handed down, the mother and daughter team have never been in the same facility.

"I hope you rot in hell," said Colleen Muller, Heiman's daughter, looking Opel right in the eyes after the verdict was read. Her brother, Greg Heiman, called Opel "a monster" and "an evil piece of trash."

The siblings also defended their father against the claim that he was an alcoholic, stating that while Heiman had his quirks and "liked his beer, hot cars, and women," he was never abusive.

"He liked to go out to the bars... but for all of that, he was a good man," Muller said.

Maintaining distance

Opel said she still can't describe what went on the night Heiman was killed.

"It's hard to explain how I felt, but I know it was a feeling I never felt before," she said. "It was like I was in some different world."

Heather, on the other hand, has spent a lot of her time in prison reliving the past – thinking back to the night of April 13, 2001. She works out, plays basketball, visits with her grandmother, and reads John Grisham novels, but she can't escape what she did to Jerry Heiman.

"I'd give up my life right now for Jerry to come back, I seriously would," she said. "I always wanted to be famous and be in the newspaper and on TV and stuff, but not like this. I guess my wish did come true – but it had a bad ending to it."

However, she has been able to reconnect with her father while in prison.

"It was a part of my heart that was missing," said Heather. "Everybody in here was like, 'oh yeah, my dad is coming to see me,' and I was thinking, 'yeah, you're so lucky to have a dad.'"

Opel attempted to reach out to her daughter as well, with a written plea from her prison cell in 2013, to be allowed to exchange letters with Heather. Her request was denied, however, by Superior Court Judge Thomas Wynne, who said he was "familiar with the case."

According to deputy prosecutor Chris Dickenson, the ruling was appropriate.

"The last time these two had regular contact," he said, "a man got murdered."

While Heather said her love for her mother remains, their relationship is considerably more complicated after Opel persuaded her to commit a murder.

"In front of the love, there is a whole bunch of hate," she said. "I know that's a strong word, but there's a whole bunch of that."

PORN STAR & KILLER : THE TRUE STORY OF AMANDA LOGUE

28

ALISON YALE

"I own a lingerie and tanning store. I also host lingerie shows. I will do almost any photo shoot but no porno films. I am fun and energetic. I am looking for paid work." - Amanda' Logue's on-line modeling profile

Amanda Logue had a double life. She was married with a young daughter. But only her husband knew what she was doing on the side to earn money.

Prostitution. Pornography.

She headlined several adult films under the stage name of "Sunny Dae". Together with her bisexual partner, Jason Andrews, the two would reach heights of sexual perversion that would lead them down the path to the ultimate taboo.

Murder.

They would rob and kill tattoo shop owner Dennis "Scooter" Abrahamsen in a shocking crime that made national headlines.

But their motivation wasn't money.

They committed the crime because it made them "hot."

EARLY LIFE

Amanda Dailey was born in the small town of Leesburg, Georgia. Her life goals were simple. She wanted "the two and a half kids, the big house and the wrap around porch. Just have the perfect life."

But things went south for Amanda in her teen years. She got pregnant during her senior year and dropped out of school to have a baby girl. Then her mother would die suddenly the following year.

She would get involved in drugs when her mom died. She would also claim that her daughter's father was abusive.

Things were a mess with numerous domestic interventions by the police.

But that is when she met police officer Lamon Logue. Logue was thirty-years old and eight years the senior of Amanda. The two hit it off as he appeared to be her knight in shining armor.

They began dating and Amanda took a shot at living the normal life. They would go to nice restaurants and to the movies. She found a job at a local car dealership as a secretary. Together, they could work together and create the American Dream.

"Lamon was clearly a good man," forensic psychologist Paula Orange said. "But he was one of those men who fall prey to the charms of a beautiful woman who is down on her luck. They feel the need to fix the woman, the need to be that knight in shining armor but in the end that narrative never works."

Amanda had an itch for more than a domesticated life with a husband and kids. Sure, she wanted a family but something was missing. Some indefinable sense of fun and fulfillment that she wasn't getting at home. Finally, her husband asked her what her lifetime dream was.

Always considered attractive, the bleach-blonde Amanda did not hesitate in answering. She always wanted to be a model.

Lamon encouraged Amanda to pursue her dreams. She answered a few ads and eventually was featured in a small advertising flyer. It was easy, quick money and Amanda enjoyed the work. Gaining more experience, she would get gig after gig and soon the money she was earning through modeling exceeded her salary at the car dealership.

ANOTHER WRONG TURN

Lamon remained the primary breadwinner despite Amanda's blossoming career and their finances took a hit when he was seriously injured in a car accident. The injuries were so severe that he had to go on disability.

Over the following months, the couple needed money. Desperately.

Amanda decided to pursue modeling assignments that were on the seedy side. She claims she simply got "swept up" by the lifestyle as she would be hired for nude photo shoots. This escalated into foot fetish jobs followed by bondage spreads.

Going down a slippery slope, she started having sex with other men on camera. Amanda was now a porn star. The money was easy and quick.

"For one shoot it would only take an hour," Amanda said. "And you could get paid thousands of dollars."

"Like most young women," Orange said. "Amanda saw performing in pornographic videos as an easy way to make cash. But Amanda was a bit older. A twenty-eight year old woman knows exactly what she's doing. It wasn't like she was some naïve eighteen-year-old from Kansas. Amanda had these desires knocking around in her head for a long time. In looking at the clips of her movies, you can see she knows exactly what she's doing. She's enjoying it. She did all of these things because she enjoyed it, whether it was drugs or having sex on camera for money."

By the end of 2007, she was appearing regularly under the name of "Sunny Dae".

Kristen Cameron, a Florida-based model who once worked with Amanda, described her as a "decent person".

"She was professional, prompt, and seemed all around normal," Cameron recalled. "She was nice to me and was a great model! I felt a connection to her since we both have southern backgrounds."

Lamon did not want to know the intimate details of what took place at the shoots. The couple needed money so he looked the other way. But the dual lifestyle began to take its toll on Amanda and once again the couple faced rock bottom.

Amanda told Lamon that she didn't want to do porn anymore. Lamon simply shrugged his shoulders and asked what can we do right now? His disability checks had not come in yet and they were pressed for cash.

Amanda would continue on in the porn business. She would accept a job in New York City for a company called Forbidden Gems.

It would be here that she would meet the man who would change her life forever.

Jason Andrews.

CON ARTIST AND GAY PORN STAR

Andrews worked as a disc jockey in Chicago and was known in the techno club scene as DJ Veritas. He was described as "obnoxious" and "brash", bragging about his military service in the United States Marines. He told everyone he was raised in Britain but was born in Israel.

Jason was popular among the velvet clubs of Chicago's Lakeview neighborhood, near Wrigley Field. He stated in his online bio that his music was based in the "grittiness of his UK elector roots." He talked with an exaggerated British accent and showed off a chiseled physique on his social media pages.

"He had girls and boys all around him," George Zelichowski said, a nightlife photographer. "They all just sort of fawned over him."

He also had a double life as a gay porn star.

Jason was reportedly straight but filed the homosexual scenes for the money, a term known as "gay for pay."

He also had a short fuse and would become "bitter or upset for no apparent reason."

He told Zelichowski that he had seen people killed ruing his time in the military but he would just stare off into the distance before going into detail.

"I have post-traumatic stress disorder," Andrews said. "Some of us know how to hide it pretty well."

During the film shoot for Forbidden Gems, Amanda because enamored with Andrews. She liked his accent and his charisma.

"The scene was that he was my boyfriend," Amanda said. "I never cared for any other partners. It was fake. This was fake. But my scenes with him were not. I liked his accent. He seemed so perfect."

The producers of the porn shoot took note that Amanda and Jason had become fast friends. They took their cigarette breaks together and slept in the same bed after filming had wrapped for the day. With the job now complete, both Andrews and Amanda decided to stay in New York for a little while longer.

RETURNING HOME

Lamon could sense the change in Amanda when she returned home. He wanted to repair the marriage. His disability checks were now coming in and he informed her that she no longer had to work in adult films.

He didn't realize, however, that Amanda found a new lover.

She would e-mail and text Andrews every day. She wanted out of the marriage.

Amanda went back home and took her daughter to her father's home in Florida. She then went to live with Jason Andrews much to her husband's dismay.

Lamon wanted to save his marriage but his wife would not hear it. She had once again descended down the path of darkness, this time she was accompanied by a man who gave her everything she wanted.

Drugs and sex.

With Andrews, Amanda only lived for the moment. The two used prescription drugs to fuel their marathon sex sessions at night. For money, Andrews continued working as a gay porn star. Amanda would work as a masseuse who would provide her clients with "happy endings."

The end goal for both was simply to get enough money to get high and have sex.

"There was passion," Amanda said. "We played around more. We talked more."

Lamon would come home to find Amanda packing her bags with a man he had never seen before.

Jason Andrews.

Lamon demanded to know what the hell was going on. Amanda brushed him off while Jason threatened to kill Lamon. He pulled a gun on his lover's husband and police were called.

"She's my wife!" Laman screamed at Andrews. "She's my wife, you piece of shit!"

Police would arrive and Laman would be humiliated in front of his former comrades. Cuckolded by a man with a British accent while his wife stuck up for her new lover.

Lamon was a nice man. He wanted to protect and provide for Amanda and her daughter. He thought these desires would be enough to entice Amanda to stay on the straight and narrow.

But with Jason, Amanda had drugs, sex, and danger.

"Jason would talk about other people's pain," Amanda said. "Going around and hurting someone. He wanted to do more than just play act. That is what got him off. Raping someone or killing someone."

"The perverse sex they engaged in was like a gateway drug," Orange said. "They needed something more and more extreme in order to get the same 'high' as they did before. Simulated rape would become real rape. Simulated killing would become real killing. They were on a slippery slope to oblivion and neither was very bright to begin with."

THE WAGES OF SIN

Dennis "Scooter" Abrahamsen wanted to have some fun.

He owned his own towing truck but had many other jobs on the side. He loved the strip clubs and worked as a bouncer there. Overweight with a sizable gut hanging over his belt, Scooter made his living primarily as a tattoo artist. When he had extra money, he would have female companions, strippers, come over to his home to entertain him. His neighbors reported seeing the young women coming and going out of his house whenever payday hit.

He was hanging out with another couple when he received a text from a woman he knew only as "Sunny Dae". She wanted to know if they could 'hang out'.

Never one to turn down a party, Scooter agreed. He went to the local 7-11 to get some cigarettes with the couple and returned home to prepare for the 'sex party' with the blonde porn star.

But Amanda had something other than a happy ending in mind for Scooter.

She texted Jason Andrews before she went to the party, detailing plans of how they would rob and kill Scooter.

Amanda arrived at the home and annoyed the other couple as she had her attention riveted to her Blackberry, texting Jason.

"They are fucked up doubt they going to-" Amanda texted.

"And him? Drunk or coked up?" Jason replied.

"Not sure yet drunk I know"

"Gotcha. Ill try and get comfy. May be here a bit!"

"Yep"

"Christ-I took another half so I can be patient! Dont worry theres anorher bar (Xanax tablet)"

'That's ok drink we can get more baby I' got some vynil gloves'

"I'm so glad you're really committed to this take. Keep eyes for a knife, etc for me! You badass. Sunrise comes quick round here."

Amber would reply back in a long, rambling text.

The talk and anticipation of killing Scooter made her "hot". She couldn't wait to kill the man and then have sex with Andrews after. The adrenaline rush got her excited.

The other couple would finally leave at 5 a.m in the morning. Amanda stayed behind and told Scooter to get on the massage table.

Jason Andrews rolled up in his car outside Scooter's home.

"Just get him on his face either bash or tell me to get in and. Where to go," Andrews texted.

"K I'm horny! I'm getting him to play music," Amber texted back.

"Wicked. I'll be waiting. Really. Take. Your. Time."

KILLING TIME

Jason would enter the home with a sledgehammer in hand and smash the unsuspecting Scooter over the head. He would hit him over a dozen times, splattering blood across the room.

Not satisfied that he was dead, Jason took a knife from the kitchen drawer and stabbed Scooter in the back over thirty times. He then took the murder weapons and dumped them in a laundry basket next to his victim.

The couple would then steal everything they could get their hands on. His laptop computer. Prescription drugs. Six thousand dollars in cash. Credit cards. A digital camera.

Fueled by drugs and adrenaline, Amanda and Jason drove to their hotel room where they had sex.

A day after the murder, Amber had messaged Jason's Twitter name 'Hearveritas' : "Taking it easy with hearveritas! Laying around eating popcorn and watching movies!"

Jason then went on the Twitter account himself and tweeted. "therealsunnydae and I wanna go watch a movie tonight, any suggestion?"

After the movie, they would go to a Home Depot in the next county over and use Scooter's credit card.

Scooter's body would not be discovered until that evening. His cousin Vincent Rella became worried that Scooter was not answering his texts. He went to Scooter's home and knocked on the door.

"I knew something was wrong," Rella said. "He would always answer the door for me."

Rella would enter the home and see his cousin laying face down, the room splattered with his blood.

It was a sight he would never forget.

The police initially thought that Scooter's murder could be a revenge killing. They knew that Scooter operated on the other side of the law sometimes. He hung out with strippers. Biker gangs. He repossessed cars.

This could be a case of someone killing him to get some payback.

Seeing the cop cars around the residence, the couple that had hung out with Scooter earlier decided to find out what was going on.

They informed the police of what took place at the home that night. They had been hanging out at a strip club called the Brass Flamingo with Scooter until he received a text from a woman named Sunny Dae.

All they knew was that she was a porn star.

They met at Scooter's home for the sex party, having intercourse in the hot tub. The couple noted that Sunny Dae looked bored and preoccupied throughout.

They left in the morning, leaving Scooter alone with the woman.

Investigators found Scooter's cell phone and traced his last calls. Interestingly, they did not find the number belonging to Amanda.

They found a number belonging to Jason Andrews.

Running a background check on Andrews, they discovered that he had been picked up for shoplifting earlier in the day with a blonde woman.

Her name was Amanda Logue, aka Sunny Dae.

Police interrogated both. They believed that Amanda was the killer and that Jason may have been a witness. Amanda remained guarded throughout the questioning. She was cool and calm, asking for a lawyer when the questions became too hot.

Jason chafed under the questioning. His hot temper flared when he was asked a simple question.

The couple posted bond and were released, however, as police didn't have enough evidence to keep them. They did have enough to get a search warrant for Amanda's white Ford Explorer. Inside, they found two different blackberry phones. The batteries and sim cards had been removed but they still hoped to be able to retrieve the messages by contacting Amanda's cell phone carrier.

With the heat now on, Amanda decided to part ways with Jason. She would return home to Leesburg, Georgia and beg forgiveness from Lamon.

Lamon would drive five hours to pick Amanda up. He had not heard from her in over three months but still loved her.

Once home, Amanda told Lamon bits and pieces of what happened. Lamon simply responded by hugging his wife.

"I told him after we got home," Amanda said. "He just held me."

She went to church that Sunday. She begged God for forgiveness.

But the investigators paid her a visit later that day, as detectives came to her home to question her about Scooter's murder.

Amanda would lie, telling him that Andrews killed him in a jealous rage after seeing her in the hot tub with him. She said that Andrews got all of the evidence, bloody knives, the hammer and surgical gloves and put them in a blue laundry basket.

Lamon thought his wife was only a murder witness. He immediately demanded to see a lawyer. But the detectives pressed the issue. It was in her best interest to tell the truth about what happened.

Amanda decided to try and save her own skin. She told police that Jason had "grabbed the back of her hair then twisted her arm behind her back." He then forced her to look at Scooter's crushed skull. He threatened her saying "that's what is going to happen to you if you tell anyone."

Amanda's story was convincing. She laid out all the narratives of an abused girlfriend. Jason had seduced her with this hedonistic lifestyle but then turned violent. Scared for her life, she didn't know what to do.

And Jason was distraught when Amanda left him. He would write on his Twitter account (in Hebrew language) : amanda please let me know if you are ok, really. My heart can't take the weight of the fear that I would never see you again."

But evidence technicians were able to recover the full extent of the text messages between Amanda and Jason. The messages were not deleted when she threw away the sim cards. They remained in the cell phone's memory chip.

The text messages were incriminating. Police immediately converged on Amanda's home.

She was more than a little surprised when they told her she was under arrest.

Amanda's demeanor of a tearful victim quickly changed. She cursed the arresting officer and began screaming at Lamon, telling him what to do.

It was further humiliation for the former cop.

Jason, meanwhile, remained at large.

It took two months but finally a tip from his current girlfriend led to his arrest. She googled his name and found out that he was wanted for murder.

He had left the Florida area and had found work in Chattanooga, Tennessee as a manager in a billiards club.

Police arrived at the club and found the British-accented Don Juan dressed like a cast member from Miami Vice.

He was shocked that they found him and told him he was under arrest.

A CON MAN FROM THE START

Jason was presented with all of the evidence and immediately cracked. He had been faking his British accent all along. He was an American citizen born and raised in Kansas. He reinvented himslef after his marriage ended in divorce.

Everything about Jason Andrews was fake.

Everything except the murder he committed.

"I was the one who swung the hammer," Andrews said. "More than a dozen times. I smashed his head in. I wasn't even shaking. I was a lot calmer than I am now. He was immediately knocked unconscious. I think that he didn't feel a thing after that. I pray that he didn't feel a thing. I really do."

Andrews asked for the death penalty.

"I deserve it," he said.

Pressed further, he had a different story to tell about Amanda. He wasn't abusing her. She was there for the fun of it.

"The motivation was robbery," Andrews said. "But if I have to be honest I think it was more about killing the man."

The excitement of murdering someone gave both Andrews and Amanda a sexual thrill.

Amanda had even texted Jason while she was having sex with Scooter in the hot tub, telling him how she couldn't wait for them to be together after the deed was done.

On July 21st, 2010, both Andrews and Amanda would be indicted on first-degree murder charges. The death penalty would be forthcoming.

Jason Andrews would reverse his initial request to be executed. Instead, he took a plea deal for life in prison. Amanda would get a 2nd-degree murder charge.

Her husband Lamon remains a faithful husband.

"I hope she'll get out," Lamon said. "She'll get out and we'll have some sort of family life."

Scooter's family, however, was not as forgiving or hopeful.

"You're not a person," Scooter's cousin, Donna Rella, said to Amanda during the trial. "He had a family. You have taken him away from us all."

"I hope anytime you close your eyes, he comes and haunts you for the rest of your pathetic life."

BONUS STORY:
AN AGGRESSIVE FLIRT

Dewayne Barrentine met Tausha Morton in early 2007.

She worked as a teacher's assistant at his son's daycare. A single parent, Barrentine would pick up his son and would be greeted by Tausha on a daily basis.

"Whenever I would pick him up," Barrentine said. "She would always make sure to step out into the hallway and give him a hug and say 'hey' to me. She made herself very noticeable."

Tausha gave Barrentine all of the hints that she was interested. The sideways glance, the smile that lingered just a little too long. But still, he needed extra coaxing.

"One of her co-workers actually approached me," Barrentine recalled when a woman in the hallway had passed him a note.

"She said, 'It's a phone number,' I said, 'To who?' She said 'Miss Tausha and she wants you go give her a call tonight. And it started from there."

Smitten by the forward nature of the sweet-faced single mother, Barrentine fell hard.

The two began dating and began living together within a month.

"She was really there for my son...," Barrentine recalled. "I had full custody of him. He would lay in the bed next to me ... and I would hear him say his prayers and he would pray for a mama." He would soon feel the same way about Tausha's daughter, Lexie.

"We weren't dating even a month and she said, 'Will you be my daddy?' And I said, 'Baby, I'll be whatever you want me to be...'"

From that moment, Barrentine became hooked as Tausha made him feel as if she really loved him. She did all the little things from kind words to love letters.

He soon began to realize, however, that Tausha had a manipulative, lying nature.

The tall tales began to pile up. She told Barrentine that she had a "Bachelor's degree in Criminal Justice" as well as an inheritance due to her from an inhertiance.

"It was from her granddad who was a federal judge who was blinded by a battery blowing up in his face. If he was a federal judge, surely his name would be on docs under Google somewhere, but I never found anything."

Barrentine grew increasingly suspicious with Tausha's stories. He did some online investigating and discovered that she had a previous marriage with a man named Mitch Kemp. He confronted her about it and she would state that she had been married five times before.

The two vaguely resembled each other, big Southern boys, "teddy bears" that were more than a little overweight.

After eight months of co-habitation, Barrentine caught Tausha cheating on him.

He promptly threw her out of his home.

"I called the Sheriff's department," Barrentine recalled. "I was like, 'look, I don't care what y'all do with her, she's got to get her shit and get outta my house.'"

Wanting retribution of some sort, Barrentine accessed Tausha's MySpace account as he knew her password.

"Dewayne gets on her Myspace account basically to mess with her," prosecutor Richard Hicks said.

After sifting through her e-mails, Barrentine would make a shocking discovery.

"I found two or three e-mails," Barrentine said. "And they were from Mitch Kemp's sister-in-law."

Mischele Kemp had written Tausha an e-mail with the subject "We're really concerned."

"How is Mitch doing? We haven't heard from you in over our year? We would like to hear from you. If we don't hear from you immediately we will contact law enforcement and media. It is not like Mitch to disappear

for years on end without contacting his mother and we have became extremely concerned. Please contact us. We are very worried about him and your entire family. Sincerely, MK."

Digging a little deeper, Barrentine looked into Tausha's "sent message" box and it did not appear that she had ever responded.

"Immediately, I changed the password on the account," Barrentine said. "To where she couldn't access it and I printed off all those e-mails."

His actions would prove to be something bigger than a missing persons case. He would bring all of this information to the local police chief in Florida who instructed him to keep things to himself as he sorted things out with the Boone County Sheriff's Department in Missouri.

WHO WAS TAUSHA MORTON?

Tausha Morton, AKA Tausha Fields, met Mitch Kemp in 2001 when she lived in Colombia, Missouri.

Mitch worked as a carpet installer and had been recently divorced after fourteen years of marriage.

"It wasn't long after he got divorced that he met Tausha," Mitch's brother Rick said. "I would say within months."

Despite their eleven year age difference, Kemp fell hard for the young and vivacious Tausha.

Tausha was the proverbial "people person." Most of her friends and neighbors described her as someone who would make you welcome and treat you as if you were a long lost friend.

"She was bubbly," said one of Tausha's former employers. "Friendly and inquisitive. She paid attention and asked lots of questions about you."

Tausha liked learning about other people. She, in turn, would be all too willing to share details of her own struggles.

"She told us how her whole family was killed in a car accident," Rick Kemp said.

Tausha had a way of getting people to feel sorry for her. She would come across as a heavily burdened individual who suffered a lot of tragedy. People listening to her story would feel compassion for her lot in life and do what they could to help her.

Mitch Kemp listened intently to Tausha's tales of woe, buying them hook, line and sinker. He wanted to help her. To be her rescuer, her knight in shining armor.

The two began to date and by September of 2002, Tausha gave birth to a baby girl.

Mitch loved kids and was ecstatic. He proposed marriage and Tausha accepted.

"They got married in Pensacola," Rick said. "It was a very easy wedding."

The marriage seemed to look okay from all observers. Mitch's family didn't have any misgivings about Tausha, her charm enabling her to get into their good graces, at least at first.

"She was a really sweet girl," Carole Kemp said, recalling her first meeting with Tausha.

But over time, his family began to notice a personality change in Mitch. Sister Mischelle stated that he wasn't "as playful as he used to be."

Family gatherings would "take a back seat to things that she wanted to do" according to Tracy Kemp, who blamed Tausha's ability to manipulate.

As work responsibilities increased for Mitch, things began to go south in their marriage very fast.

DOMESTIC LIFE AIN'T FOR ME

Bored that she was left alone with the baby, the high-strung Tausha needed an outlet.

She would arrive at her friend's gym, the Body Zone, with her baby in tow. Soon she began working part time at the fitness center.

It was there that she would meet Greg Morton.

Morton was more physically fit than Kemp but he fit the same profile psychologically. He had recently broken up with a longtime girlfriend and was be vulnerable to the manipulative charms of Tausha.

"Greg was despondent over his break-up," a family friend said. "But when he met Tausha, he kinda perked back up."

Tausha used the same seductive strategy on Morton as she used on Kemp. She detailed her tragic back story. She told him stories of being molested, of being raped.

She also told Morton in no uncertain terms that her marriage with Kemp was on the outs. Making herself look like the victim, she told Morton that Kemp had made her miserable. He was abusive, bothered her constantly and threatened physical harm.

"She told him a bunch of lies," one of Tausha's friends said. "She said she was getting him (Mitch) served, that they were getting divorced."

By February 2004, her allegations of physical abuse would be reported to the police department as Tausha filed assault charges against him.

"She said he abused her," Rick Kemp said. "By assaulting her, or slapping her or something."

Tausha informed police that she and Mitch had gotten into an argument. Then he hauled off and hit her.

Mitch Kemp would plead guilty to the charges and spend over a month in jail. Upon his release, he would be in for another surprise.

Tausha had moved out of the family home and moved in with Greg Morton, taking Lexie with her. Morton had own a farm outside of Colombia, Missouri, a sizable estate that he inherited from his step-father.

A custody battle then ensued between Tausha and Mitch for their daughter. The fight would get uglier by the day with daily phone calls between the two and their attorneys. She would refuse to allow Mitch to see Lexie and used the courts to prevent visitation.

But Mitch Kemp would not give up without a fight.

"If he had to go through the court system to do it, he would do it," Mitch's brother Rick said. "But that he was going to see his daughter."

Tausha would state that their divorce was finalized in August as the custody battle lingered on. She would then marry Greg Morton the same month.

But Morton had no idea what he was getting into and a "triangle" domestic dispute ensued.

Tausha had arranged to meet with Mitch in order to get some personal belongings. She drove in with Greg to the house of Mitch's friend where he was staying. Mitch confronted Tausha on the front porch where he immediately berated her, screaming insults.

Greg was waiting in the car at the time and went to intervene on Tausha's behalf. Mitch became further enraged and hit Greg over the head with a patio chair.

Retreating, Greg and Tausha sprinted back to the car.

Mitch, however, would disappear after that confrontation.

THE DISAPPEARANCE OF MITCH KEMP

It took awhile for Mitch's disappearance to hit home for his family members and friends. He was the type of man whom you would not hear from from awhile but would suddenly show up on the front porch.

He was dutiful about calling his mother Carole and when she didn't hear from him, she began to worry.

"We called the Boone County Sheriff's office," Rick Kemp said. "About two weeks afterward, probably. We told them that Mitch had disappeared."

The Sheriff's department did not think any foul play was involved. They offered assurance to the family that Mitch "probably didn't want to be found."

Boone County detectives came to that conclusion after they found out that Mitch was wanted for stealing some goods from a friend. They believed he disappeared in order to escape from repercussions of his actions.

Meanwhile, Greg and Tausha were living large. In late 2004, Greg put up his farm for sale which surprised both his friends and family. He treasured the land as it was bequeathed to him from his stepfather. Those close to him believed that Tausha had put him up to it.

In February of 2005, the sale of the farm finalized. With a $275,000 payout in hand, he and Tausha left Missouri, telling no one.

The Kemp family continued to believe that Mitch was not missing and that Tausha was involved somehow. They just didn't have any evidence or clues. Just a damn strong suspicion.

"Something had either happened to Mitch that had nothing to do with Tausha," Rick Kemp said. "Or something happened to Mitch and Tausha had something to do with it."

Both the Kemp family and Boone County law enforcement would then find locating Tausha and Greg to be a fruitless exercise. They literally disappeared from the face of the earth, wanting a new life. Leaving no trail behind, Tausha and Greg would move all the way to the Gulf Coast.

Greg, still smitten by Tausha, would get a tattoo of her name on his back as if he were a branded cow. With a new man firmly under her control, Tausha would go on a spending spree which included getting breast implants with Greg's money.

NO SIGN OF MITCH

By February of 2008, the Kemp family still had not heard from Mitch.

"They took a missing persons report," Rick Kemp said. "But the case went cold, quite frankly, because they didn't do anything about it."

But the Kemp family would not give up hope. They continued their search, turning to the Internet to look for any trace of their beloved son and brother.

They would search different social networking sites and court systems to look for any trace of Mitch.

They found nothing for years.

Until Mischelle Kemp found Tausha on MySpace, the social networking account.

"My sister-in-law found an account," Rick Kemp said. "That had Tausha's name and picture on it."

Mischelle immediately sent Tausha an e-mail.

"Tausha didn't respond," Rick Kemp said. "But Dewayne Berrentine did."

REVENGE SEEKING BOYFRIEND TO THE RESCUE

Dewayne Berrentine read through Tausha's e-mails on MySpace and began connecting the dots.

"Her little stories," Berrentine said. "Just because somebody lies to me, that doesn't mean I'm going to call you out on it immediately. I thought that she was coming up with these stories to impress me, maybe?"

Dewayne had discovered that Tausha had gotten around. He received some disturbing information from a man that Tausha had dated after she met Greg and before she met Dewayne.

His name was Keith Jones.

"I was in love with her and anything else didn't matter," Jones recalled. "You couldn't verify anything that she said," he says. "You know, and I mean there were a lot of stories."

Keith and Dewayne exchanged notes and stories about Tausha. They realized that she told them the same outlandish stories. But then Jones told Dewayne a story that he didn't hear before.

He described how Tausha revealed to him that she was involved in the murder of one of her exes.

"She had a few drinks in her," Jones recalled. "She said this guy had raped her and her daughter. And she apparently ... went to where he was and lured him back to her house ... and he walked in the front door. And that's when Greg shot him in the chest."

Both men thought the story was "so far-fetched" and because of the lies they always heard from her, thought nothing of it.

Dewayne did eventually confront Tausha about the allegation and she dismissed it out of hand, saying that her ex-boyfriend would say anything to throw a wrench into her new relationship.

Dewayne would change his mind about things when he opened Mischelle Kemp's e-mail message to Tausha, however. After notifying the authorities, he also wrote Mischelle Kemp back who in turn contacted the authorities in Boone County. The Sheriff's department then reopened the case. After doing some sniffing around, they discovered that Mitch had "fallen off the face of the earth" and had not filed taxes in over four years.

Finally, the Boone County Sheriff department realized that something was wrong.

INVESTIGATING TAUSHA

Detectives decided to start researching the background of Tausha.

They would discover that Tausha's parents were alive contrary to her account that they were both dead. Mitch's mother had spoken to Tausha's father shortly before her soon was to be married.

"She said, 'Mitch, we need to talk,'" recalled Rick Kemp. "You've heard a bunch of stories. Her family wasn't killed in a car wreck. They're alive. They don't want anything to do with Tausha. They say she's nothing but trouble."

Mitch dismissed the notion of his mother. He was totally smitten with Tausha.

Further investigations would reveal that Tausha had been married and divorced twice by the time she met Mitch Kemp. She would go onto have four marriages before she was thirty and the number of men she lived were numerous. Mitch had no idea that Tausha went from one man to the next man to the next. Even if he did, he was so smitten by her early in their relationship that he would have probably ignored the red flags.

Investigators would further discover that her divorce to Kemp was never finalized so she may have married Greg Morton while she was still married to Kemp.

Tracking her movements after she moved from Missouri proved difficult. Tausha and Greg were eventually tracked to Alabama.

The couple lived an indulgent lifestyle, buying luxury homes and cars on the $275,000 sale they profited after selling the farm.

But it didn't take long for them to blow through the money.

Needing more income to support Tausha, Greg would go to Mississippi in the hopes of finding clean-up work after Hurricane Katrina hit. After he left, Tausha saw it as an opportunity to cut him loose.

She had to find someone new.

"While he was gone doing Katrina," Barrentine said. "She was blowing through his money. Then he came home finding another man laying in his bed and he's broke."

Greg would immediately file for divorce.

MEN AND MORE MEN

Cut off from her money supply from Greg, Tausha would find work as an assistant at a day care center. It was there that she would meet Dewayne Barrentine.

She would follow the same modus operandi in her seduction of Barrentine, telling him the sob stories of her life. She described how Greg Morton would abuse her and how she escaped. She gave details on how Greg would try to "jump on her" and that they had "several physical altercations."

Agreeing to let her move in, Dewayne would meet Greg when he was helping Tausha get her belongings out of his house.

The two didn't fight. Instead, they spoke briefly and Greg would later tell Dewayne about how detectives from Missouri were looking to speak with Tausha.

Barrentine would eventually discover Tausha cheating on him and throw her out of his home. She would find a new boyfriend a few days later by the name of Denver Workman.

Workman left his job and his extended family from Florida to Wilmington, Delaware after Tausha begged him to do so. Then she wanted him to move back and Workman refused.

"She would yell, scream and throw things at me because I wasn't leaving," Workman recalled. "She would tell Lexie I was a bad person and to kick me. I bought her a bus ticket to Florida and let her borrow my truck that was still down there. She took the truck, and I never saw her again."

Police would finally catch up to Tausha in Dothan, Alabama and confront her about the disappearance of Mitch Kemp.

During her initial interrogation, Tausha would firmly deny having any contact with Mitch.

"What do you mean what happened to Mitch?" Tausha would ask detectives in bewilderment. "I haven't had any contact with him. None."

The investigators continued to press, however, and Tausha would try to insinuate Greg as having something to do with Mitch's disappearance.

"They had words on the phone," Tausha told detectives. "And then they had, they got in a fist fight one time."

After being threatened with the possibility of being put in jail and leaving her five year old daughter Lexie in the hands of the state, Tausha then placed the blame on Greg.

"Greg killed Mitch," Tausha said. "He told me."

She would then inform detectives that she wasn't there when it happened. She stated that Greg left about 45 minutes later after he had yet another phone conversation with Mitch.

Tausha would claim that she feared for both her and her child's life because of Greg's temper.

She would recall that Greg shot Mitch on the farm. Investigators played along, even paying for her plane ticket to fly from Alabama to Missouri in order to let them know where Greg had buried Mitch. But once she arrived, Tausha seemed confused by the layout of the farm. She could not pinpoint where exactly the body had been buried.

She was then released under her own recognizance back to Alabama while Sheriff deputies proceeded to dig up the farm to no avail. They used ground penetrating radar, cadaver sniffing dogs but came up empty.

WHERE WAS GREG MORTON?

While talks with Tausha revealed some clues, investigators were even more eager to speak with Greg Morton.

After ending his marriage with Tausha, he settled in St. Louis. He was going to school to become an electrician and had a new girlfriend.

He wanted nothing further to do with Tausha. When investigators approached him, Greg immediately invoked his right to an attorney and refused to speak further.

Detectives did not have enough evidence to charge him. But they had Tausha on the run and spoke to her again. This go around, they decided to employ a little psychological manipulation.

"But I tell you what," Detective Dave Wilson said while sitting across from Tausha in the interrogation room. "He (Greg Morton) automatically assumed that you talked to us. Now, we didn't confirm that."

"Why did he think that?" Tausha asked.

"Well, there's only...who knows?"

"But he said he thought he'd talk to you?"

"I'm going to ask you again. Can you take us directly to where that hole was?"

This go around, Tausha said yes. The Boone County Sheriff's department flew her in from Alabama yet again to Greg Morton's farm.

This time, Tausha led investigators straight to where the body was buried.

Mitch Kemp's remains were dug up and his identity was confirmed.

"It didn't surprise us," Rick Kemp said. "But we were all just blown away. I mean, I just didn't want to believe that my brother was gone."

Investigators discovered that Mitch had been shot numerous times and found numerous shell casings in the makeshift grave. They then went to St. Louis and arrested Greg Morton.

"He wasn't surprised when we showed up," Detective Wilson recalled.

Tausha was allowed to return home but investigators had a suspicion that she was more involved than she let on.

A VOW OF SILENCE

Greg strangely refused to rat out Tausha, remaining in prison until he was officially charged.

Tausha moved to Texas, however, and began dating someone new. Investigators would catch up with her again, however, and this time a heated ninety-minute interrogation would ensue.

Their probing questions would force Tausha to change her story about Mitch's murder completely.

"I did not do anything," Tausha said after detectives informed her that she would be charged with first-degree murder. "I helped you in every way I could possibly fucking help you.

"Tausha," Detective Wilson said slowly. "We got people who say, say otherwise, okay."

Tausha then changed her story again, stating that she was present when Greg murdered Mitch.

"I snuck around behind Greg's back and I saw Mitch, okay," Tausha said. "Greg had no idea."

She stated Greg would kill Mitch in a jealous rage after they returned from a hotel for a tryst. They then drove back to the farm and Greg assaulted Mitch before he got out of the car.

"He had a gun in his hands," Tausha said. "It was a black gun. Mitch started walking backwards. I ran inside the house and then I ran back outside. I saw that Mitch was walking backwards, and Greg was walking towards him. And Greg shot him. I didn't kill Mitch. I didn't want Mitch to die."

But the investigators didn't see it that way. They charged her with first-degree murder.

THE TRIAL

In June of 2009, Tausha had been imprisoned for over six months as she awaited trial.

Her bail was set at one million dollars.

Greg Morton then decided it was time to cut a deal. He broke his silence on what really happened the day of Mitch Kemp's murder. He would admit to his involvement in exchange for a more lenient sentence if he testified against Tausha.

In 2010, Tausha's trial began.

The prosecution's argument was that Tausha was the mastermind behind the murder, that even though Greg pulled the trigger it was Tausha that put the idea in his head. They also believed that Tausha's motive was to have sole custody of their daughter.

The defense would claim that Tausha was innocent and the victim. Her attorney was, in essence, using the same technique that Tausha used on all of her men. They would play on sympathy and hope that the jury would be as charmed by Tausha as all of her men.

GREG MORTON CONFESSES

Morton would take the stand and tell the jury exactly how Tausha manipulated him to kill Mitch.

"She's hysterical," Morton recalled. "She said Mitch raped her."

"What are you feeling, Greg, at this point?" Prosecutor Hicks asked.

"I wanted retribution. Tausha took charge and handed me a gun the net morning. She goes, 'I'm going to get Mitch, and when I get back, you shoot him.'"

"What were you going to do, Greg?"

"I was going to do what she asked me to do."

"They made a plan in that Tausha was going to go in town and pick Mitch up," Rick Kemp said. "And tell him that Greg was out of town."

Mitch arrived at the farm, thinking that it would only be the two of them. But then Greg emerged from the porch.

"I had a gun in my hand," Morton recalled. "I raised it and pointed it at him. I kinda paused I was kinda struggling with it a little bit. And then she started yelling at me to shoot him."

Greg believed that he was committing a protective act. He believed that Mitch was raping Tausha and molesting their six-year-old daughter.

"Then she said 'You got to get something to move him. Get something to move him with." Greg recalled. "Then she said, 'Come on. You should have had this ready.'"

"And you saw that she was still struggling?"

"He was."

"So what did you do?"

"I shot him again."

"Was he struggling anymore?"

"It was over," Morton said. "I used farm equipment to pick up Mitch's body and we buried him in a pit. When we were rolling the dirty on Mitch she said 'Mitch Kemp is a piece of shit and nobody is going to look for him for a long time.'"

The defense would then call a neighbor who testified on Tausha's behalf, stating that she thought she was under Greg's control.

Greg then broke down on the stand and tearfully apologized to Mitch Kemp's family.

Over time, however, he began to realize that Tausha was a cunning liar. As he got to know her better, he realized that he had been duped.

"He'd been played like a fiddle by her," Rick Kemp said. "She did it to every man that she had."

Tausha was not called to the stand by the defense and the jury would find her guilty.

"I think she thought she was going to walk," Rick Kemp said. "She thought she could just get away with lying and manipulating people."

Tausha Morton was sentenced to life in prison without parole but is currently appealing her sentencing.

bonus story:

Christa Gail Pike, born 10 March 1976, currently sits on Tennessee's death row for the murder of Colleen Slemmer, 19, on 12 January 1995. The murder occurred when Pike was 18 years old. Pike and her then-boyfriend Tadaryl Shipp who was 17 at the time of the murder were convicted of Slemmer's murder and conspiracy to commit murder. Another friend of the defendants and the victim, Shadolla Peterson, also 18 at the time, was convicted as an accessory after the fact and given six years' probation after turning informant. Pike was sentenced to death by electrocution in 1996 and, at the time, she had the distinction of being the youngest woman ever to be sentenced to death, in any state and only the second women given the death penalty in Tennessee.

Early Life

Pike's life reads like a primer for depraved murderers. As a small child, Pike did not enjoy a healthy and supportive bond with her mother, Carissa Hansen, a licensed nurse, allegedly because of her premature birth. Whereas thousands of children are born prematurely and do not resort to criminal behavior Pike's birth was presented as evidence of one possible origin of her poor and troubled behavior. Pike's maternal grandmother was verbally abusive and Pike was raised by her alcoholic and abusive paternal grandmother until the latter's death in 1988 when Pike was 12; after which Pike attempted suicide by overdosing. She was then shuttled back and forth between her divorced parents' homes. In 1989, Pike was kicked out of her father's house for the second and final time due to her unruliness and the alleged sexual abuse of her father's then-two-year old daughter with his second wife.

Prior to the murder, experts assert that there were myriad indications that Pike was seriously disturbed; however, nobody who may have suspected this sought help for the increasingly disobedient and incorrigible young lady. According to Pike's mother, she was problematic since the age of eight and the two of them had a contentious relationship due to Pike's fluctuating and troubling behavior. Her mother asserted that by age nine Pike was growing marijuana in pots at their home and had been permitted to have a live-in boyfriend at age 14. At one point—in an effort to improve their relationship—Hansen suggested that she and Pike smoke marijuana together. Hansen mistakenly believed that cultivating a friendship with her daughter would cultivate the necessary bond Pike had been lacking her entire life. At one point, one of her mother's boyfriends whipped Pike with a belt which prompted her to wield a butcher knife against him before he was subsequently arrested. Hansen also admitted that Pike had repeatedly lied to and stolen from her. In several interviews with Hansen throughout Pike's trial and seemingly endless appeals, she admitted repeatedly that she was a terrible mother and should have spent more time with her daughter.

Pike's aunt, Carrie Ross, provided insight into Pike's upbringing when she testified that she disallowed her own children from associating with Pike because she lived in a filthy house that had zero ground rules and that Pike was a pathological liar of whom she was somewhat afraid. She also admitted that there was a history of substance abuse in Pike's family. Ross also stated that on the few occasions that Pike actually visited her she behaved like a little girl and engaged in Barbie and dress-up play with her eleven-year-old cousin. Further, there were some allegations that Pike may have been sexually abused but these were neither confirmed nor denied.

Pike's father, Glenn Pike testified that he did, in fact, kick his daughter out of his house multiple times; the last time being in 1989 after the aforementioned allegations that Pike sexually abused her two-year old half-sister. He admitted that he had signed adoption papers for Pike prior to her 18th birthday and that during the times she resided with him she was manipulative, disobedient, and dishonest.

After dropping out of high school, Pike began Job Corps classes in computer programming. Job Corps is a government-based organization that provides occupational and vocational training to underprivileged and troubled teens. It was at the now-defunct Job Corps center in Knoxville where she met Shipp, Slemmer, and Peterson. While Job Corps seeks to promote prosocial behavior and foster a strong desire among its participants to learn a vocation and secure a more promising future than might have been previously the case, this program is also known to cultivate criminal activity, likely due to the association among its participants; many of whom already had problematic behavior.

Evidence of Premeditation

On 11 January 1995, the day before the actual homicide, Pike told friend and co-Job Corps student Kim Iloilo that she was planning to kill Slemmer because she "just felt mean that day." Iloilo discounted Pike's statement as nothing more than merely talk; however, the following evening at approximately 8:00 p.m. Iloilo witnessed Pike, Shipp, Peterson, and Slemmer leaving the Job Corps center. When Iloilo saw Pike, Shipp, and Peterson returning at approximately 10:15 p.m. without Slemmer she, again, thought nothing of it. Even when Pike visited Iloilo's dorm room at 11:00 p.m. that night and confessed to killing Slemmer—as well as showing Iloilo what Pike identified as a piece of Slemmer's skull—Iloilo still failed to tell anyone. Later, at Pike's trial, Iloilo testified that while Pike was iterating the events of the murder she was oddly smiling, singing, and dancing around the room. The following morning Iloilo asked Pike what she was going to do with the piece of skull. Pike nonchalantly replied that she had it in her pocket and was, in fact, eating breakfast with it.

Pike also told another student, Stephanie Wilson, a similar account the following day and proudly described the brown spots on her shoes as blood. Not unlike Iloilo, Wilson failed to immediately report anything.

The Crime Scene

On 13 January, officers from the University of Tennessee and Knoxville Police Departments were dispatched to greenhouses on the University's agricultural campus in Tyson Park where a University grounds department employee reported finding, at approximately 8:05 a.m., what he assumed to be a dead animal. The gruesome discovery was a corpse that turned out to be Colleen Slemmer. She was naked from the waist up; her throat was cut; her head had been bludgeoned; and she had various cuts all over her arms, throat, and torso—including a pentagram that had been carved into her chest. Officer John Terry Johnson who testified at Pike's trial described Slemmer's body as so badly beaten that she was unrecognizable as a human being. He also stated that he thought he was looking at her face when, in reality,

Slemmer was lying face-down in the dirt and debris where Pike, Shipp, and Peterson had left her.

There was additional evidence and testimony that the crime scene encompassed an area that measured 100 feet long by 60 feet wide; an astounding 6,000 square feet in area. Despite the area being muddy and wet there was ample evidence of a physical struggle with trampled bushes, a considerable amount of blood, body drag marks, and hand and knee prints. Thirty feet from Slemmer's body was a large pool of blood which suggested that Slemmer was attacked in one area and then dragged to where her body was later found. Slemmer's shirt and bra were also discovered at the crime scene, as well as a bloody rag that Pike admitted to tying over Slemmer's mouth at one point to keep her from screaming.

Disturbingly, University of Tennessee police officer Harold James Underwood, Jr., who was the officer assigned to secure the crime scene, testified at trial that Pike and a few other females came to the scene between four and five p.m. the day of the discovery and before Pike was even considered to be a suspect. Underwood stated that Pike had asked why the wooded area was marked off, who the victim was, and whether police had any leads as to who the suspect or suspects were. He particularly recalled Pike's odd behavior—moving around a lot while giggling amusedly—and that she wore a necklace in the shape of a pentagram. The following day, during briefing when informed that the victim had a pentagram carved into her chest, Underwood reported Pike's behavior and necklace to his supervisors.

Autopsy and Findings

During Slemmer's autopsy, the medical examiner, Dr. Sandra Elkins, had to identify the victim's body from dental records because her head was so bludgeoned that she was unrecognizable. After cleaning up Slemmer's body which was clad only in jeans, socks, and shoes, and covered with dirt and twigs, Dr. Elkins began cataloging Slemmer's wounds. Due to the sheer number of wounds on her back, arms, abdomen, and chest, and the fact that following department policy which stated that each individual wound be assigned a letter of the alphabet, when Dr. Elkins reached double letters she, instead, individually catalogued only the most serious wounds and that there were innumerable other superficial and defensive wounds. Among the most serious cuts was a six-inch gaping wound across Slemmer's throat that was deep enough to penetrate the fat and muscles in her neck as well as the aforementioned pentagram. Additional injuries included fresh bruising which Dr. Elkins asserted was consistent with crawling.

Cause of death was ultimately attributed to blunt force trauma to the head. Dr. Elkins surmised that Slemmer's head was hit with the asphalt at least four times—two to the left side, one over the right eye, and one to the nose—which collectively resulted in multiple and extensive skull fractures. One of these blows was to the left side of Slemmer's head—which, according to Dr. Elkins, occurred with the right side of the victim's head against a firm surface. This blow only fractured her skull but also imbedded a portion of Slemmer's skull into her head and contained black particles from the piece of asphalt determined to be the murder weapon.

Even more tragic was Dr. Elkins' findings that none of Slemmer's other wounds would have rendered her unconscious and evidence of active blood flow around the wounds and blood in her sinus cavity indicated that Slemmer was alive during the severe torture she suffered before being killed.

Arrest and Confession

The police quickly connected Pike to the homicide thanks to the piece of Slemmer's skull discovered in Pike's jacket pocket. Pike had left this jacket hanging on the back of a chair in Job Corps Orientation Specialist Robert A. Pollock's office on 13 January after meeting with him about a misplaced ID card. Pike's jacket remained in Pollock's office from 4:00 p.m. on 13 January until 7:30 a.m. on 17 January. After learning over the weekend that Pike was a suspect in Slemmer's murder investigation, Pollock immediately gave the jacket to William Hudson, the Job Corps' safety and security captain who turned it over to Knoxville Police Department Officer Arthur Bohanan. At trial, Bohanan would testify that he found a small piece of bone in one of the pockets and presented it to Dr. Murray Marks, a University of Tennessee forensic anthropologist who was reconstructing Slemmer's decapitated skull and the piece in Pike's jacket pocket fit perfectly into an area where a portion of her skull was missing at the time of the victim's discovery.

When confronted with this evidence and subsequently arrested, Pike waived her *Miranda* protections and confessed to the murder and permitted officers to search her dorm room where the blood-soaked jeans she wore the previous night were found. Additionally, Pike led officers to a trash can at a nearby Texaco station on Cumberland Avenue where she had disposed of Slemmer's ID and a pair of gloves Pike had been wearing at the time of the homicide.

Pike's transcribed confession was 46 pages long.

In it, Pike admitted that there was animosity between Slemmer and her because Pike was convinced that Slemmer was a rival for the affections of her boyfriend, Shipp, and that Slemmer was trying to get Pike kicked out of the Job Corps program so she could have Shipp for herself. Pike also claimed that she had awakened one night to find Slemmer standing above her with a box cutter; however, there is no evidence of this allegation. Instead, Slemmer had repeatedly called her mother, May Martinez, to tell her she was afraid of Pike who she had awakened to find in her room and that she wanted to come home; to which Slemmer's mother said that she couldn't because she had signed a contract. Pike stated that she had only planned to fight Slemmer to stop her from running her mouth. On that fateful night of 12 January, Pike, Slemmer, Shipp, and Peterson signed the Job Corps logbook as they were leaving for an outing Slemmer believed was to smoke marijuana en route to a video store so that Pike and she could try to work out their problems.

When the group entered a tunnel at the edge of Tyson Park, Slemmer likely felt that something was not quite right and proceeded to ask Pike where they were going and whether there was, in fact, any marijuana. These questions irritated Pike who began the brutal assault shortly thereafter after they had gone deeply enough into the woods so that nobody could hear them that led to Slemmer's murder.

Pike confessed to initially slamming Slemmer's head into her knee and then throwing her to the ground where Pike continually punched, kicked, and slammed Slemmer's head into the concrete, screaming, "the bi*ch won't die" and that she wanted "to see [Slemmer's] brains flow." According to witnesses Shipp and Peterson, as Slemmer continued to plead with Pike to stop, Pike got angrier and more brutal. Slemmer offered to return to her Florida home, leave her belongings at the Job Corps center, and not tell anyone what happened; however, Pike became more enraged and yelled at Slemmer to be quiet because "it was harder to hurt someone who was talking to you."

In addition to the savage beating, Slemmer had been cut innumerable times with a box cutter and a mini meat cleaver (that Pike had allegedly borrowed from another Job Corps student) to her torso, arms, face, and back including having had her throat slit six times prior to the fatal blow that resulted from having her head crushed by a piece of asphalt. There was also a pentagram carved into Slemmer's chest; however, Pike asserted that Shipp had done that. Pike also confessed to "just watching Slemmer bleed" when the victim got up and tried to run away. Pike admitted to cutting Slemmer's back: "the big long cut."

After the murder, Pike stated that she and Shipp washed their hands and shoes in a nearby mud puddle to conceal the blood, dumped the box cutter, and Pike returned the meat cleaver to the person from which she borrowed it. This person has never been identified.

The physical evidence and co-defendant testimony suggested that the assault and murder lasted from 30 minutes to an hour and consisted of Slemmer repeatedly trying to get up and run away but was prevented from doing so by the co-defendants who also, as Pike testified, contributed to the physical assault by throwing rocks at Slemmer's head and holding her down so she couldn't run away. Later, Pike would testify that she heard voices in her head overriding Slemmer's continual screaming, telling her that she needed to prevent Slemmer from filing charges against her for attempted murder. Pike also admitted that at one point she thought she had heard a noise and went to investigate it to ensure that they were alone, as well as alleging that during the assault she heard Slemmer breathing in blood and jerking but did not let this assuage her anger as Pike continued her savagery.

Even more troublesome, a police video recorded after Pike's confession shows Pike smiling and providing extensive details about the crime at the crime scene, oftentimes mimicking her actions that evening. Many have said that her demeanor on the recording was eerily similar to that of a little girl who was excited and happy that she had experienced the best day of her life and had no problem talking about the events that transpired, the heinousness of her actions, and how she felt about it all.

The facts of the homicide are not nor have they ever been in dispute, thanks to an abundance of evidence. Pike's confession, and witness testimony at the trial.

Pre-Trial Examination

Prior to her trial, Pike was given a battery of assessment tests and examined by numerous psychiatrists including clinical psychologist Dr. Eric Engum who found her to be extremely bright as evidenced by an I.Q. of 111—in the 77th percentile of the general population—which he believed to be remarkable given her difficult childhood and lack of formal schooling beyond the ninth grade. Dr. Engum also found that

Pike had excellent reasoning, problem solving, language, and analytic skills, and was also quite adept at paying attention, sustaining concentration, and sequencing information. Dr. Engum concluded that Pike was legally sane and had no brain damage which has frequently been demonstrated to cause violent behavior in some individuals.

Of particular interest was that Pike was found to be marijuana- and inhalant-dependent and also diagnosed with borderline personality disorder. Whereas there are some similarities between borderline personality disorder and antisocial personality disorder such as impulsivity, irritability, aggression, and a self-image that fluctuates between self-aggrandizement and despair, there are several differences. Individuals with borderline personality disorder differ from those with antisocial behavior in that the former—which primarily affects females—is characterized by a lack of remorse, self-destructiveness, black-and-white thinking, alcohol and/or drug use or abuse, unstable relationships characterized by fear of abandonment and extreme swings between love and hate, difficulty in achieving academic and vocational goals, and are more likely to have been sexually abused; while the latter—which affects disproportionately more males—is characterized by a lack of affect and remorse, emptiness, and an ultimate goal of self-preservation.

Pike demonstrated all of the aforementioned characteristics of borderline personality disorder which makes it easier—but not justifiably so—to comprehend how her intense jealousy of Slemmer and fear of losing Shipp made her commit her atrocious acts. In addition to her fear of abandonment, Pike also abused drugs, was likely sexually abused, had contentious relationships, and displayed zero remorse. Dr. Engum surmised that Pike did not act with premeditation or deliberation in Slemmer's murder but, instead, in a manner that was consistent with borderline personality disorder. More simply, Pike had lost control. However, on cross-examination Dr. Engum admitted that Pike's deliberate luring of Slemmer, that she carved a pentagram in the victim's chest, that she brought weapons with her, and that she bashed Slemmer's head into the concrete does, in fact, constitute deliberateness.

That Pike was overjoyed and singing in Iloilo's room describing the murder while dancing around with the portion of Slemmer's skull Pike had taken as a trophy further supported Dr. Engum's diagnosis of borderline personality disorder because she had eliminated who she perceived was in competition for her boyfriend, Shipp, and, therefore, could continue her relationship with him. When questioned about the piece of skull Pike had taken, Dr. Engum said that Pike had no identity and her actions of taking and displaying the skull was a way to get recognition, no matter how misleading and distorted said recognition might be. In fact, after her conviction and sentencing Pike wrote a letter to Shipp which was intercepted by jail personnel that stated that even though she tried to be "nice" to Slemmer by bashing in her head instead of letting her bleed to death she was still sentenced to "fry."

The Trial

There was an abundance of evidence presented at the trial. Physical evidence consisted of crime scene photographs, autopsy reports, bloody clothing, and the piece of Slemmer's skull Pike had taken as a trophy. With respect to this skull piece, Dr. Elkins presented Slemmer's decapitated skull that was reconstructed by Dr. Marks to explain the victim's injuries. The skull presented at trial was complete except for a portion that was missing on the left side of Slemmer's skull. Dr. Elkins demonstrated that the piece of skull found in Pike's jacket fit perfectly into this spot, much to the chagrin of Slemmer's mother who, in a taped interview, stated that Pike was oftentimes giggling and passing notes to her mother and defense attorney during the trial, not unlike an immature middle-schooler.

At the trial, the State introduced photographs taken of Pike and Shipp at the Knoxville Police Department in which both were wearing pentagram necklaces similar to the shape carved into Slemmer's chest. It was presented that both Pike and Shipp dabbled in devil worshiping and other forms of the occult and that Slemmer was a sacrifice for the next day, Friday the 13th. Despite the presence of some type of satanic elements in Slemmer's murder, Dr. William Bernet, Vanderbilt University's psychiatric hospital medical director, testified that the evidence was that of "an adolescent dabbling in Satanism." He further concluded that the concept of collective aggression—or mob mentality—in which a group of people become stimulated and subsequently engage in some type of violent behavior was most assuredly at play in the events leading to Slemmer's death. However, Dr. Bernet ultimately stated that he did not have enough evidence to definitively surmise whether Pike had acted with premeditation or intent when she lured and murdered Slemmer.

Pike was ultimately convicted of first-degree murder and conspiracy to commit first-degree murder after a mere two-and-a-half hours of jury deliberation. The fact that the jury returned guilty verdicts for first-degree murder—and did it so quickly—demonstrate that jurors were convinced that Pike had the requisite mens rea, or mental capacity, to warrant a first-degree murder charge: premeditation and deliberation. Amidst the overwhelming evidence and utter lack of remorse for her actions Pike was sentenced to death by electrocution (Tennessee has since adopted lethal injection for executions but has the prerogative to utilize electrocution if the lethal injection drugs cannot be obtained). Shipp was sentenced to life without parole because his age at the time of the murder was too young to warrant capital punishment and Peterson turned informant and was given six years' probation for her testimony.

Pike's conviction was upheld by the Court of Criminal Appeals and the United States Supreme Court denied certiorari.

Post-Conviction

While incarcerated, Pike demonstrated more evidence of her depravity. In 2001 she tried to murder fellow inmate Patricia Jones by strangling her with a shoelace. Pike alleges that Jones repeatedly tortured her by calling her "fried chicken" and making various demeaning sounds as an affront to what Jones said was the sound that Pike would make when she was electrocuted. The final straw was when Jones physically threatened Pike's friend, fellow devil worshiper Natasha Cornet. Pike said that she jumped atop Jones and choked her with a shoelace so that the much larger and heavier Jones would get off of Cornet. By the time prison guards reached them, Jones was unconscious.

Pike was subsequently convicted of attempted murder despite her prior death sentence because any offense committed while an individual is incarcerated must be adjudicated. During this time, neurology specialist Dr. Jonathan Henry Pincus began investigating Pike's brain to glean some type of knowledge as to why Pike behaved and continued to act violently the way she did when she assaulted Jones. He asserted that every killer he has ever examined share three commonalities: brain damage, a history of abuse, and mental illness. Dr. Pincus alleged that Pike did, in fact, possess all three features and demonstrates all of the requisite features common to serial killers. There is much consensus among professionals that Pike would likely have been a serial killer had she not been caught the first time.

He also testified at Pike's attempted murder trial that her brain's frontal lobes are not "put together properly"; largely due, he claimed, to the fact that Pike's mother drank while she was pregnant with Pike despite denial of this by Pike's mother. It was also brought up that as a child Pike played at the slaughterhouse where her grandfather worked and that she was frequently subjected to pornography and horror movies on the home television screen. He asserted that all of these factors provide insight into how an 18-year old girl could act with such depravity as was the case when Pike murdered Slemmer.

However, the original trial judge, Mary Beth Leibowitz, stated that Pincus' "findings" of brain damage was curious as the defense expert at Pike's original trial who was trying to spare her the death penalty failed to find such evidence.

Forensic psychiatrist William Kenner testified that Pike had suffered from undiagnosed bipolar disorder, the symptoms of which were evident from the time Pike was a "sleepless, talkative adolescent" and likened her to an automobile with cruise control set at 120 miles per hour. Pike's post-conviction defense team alleged that this non-diagnosis justified her requesting a new trial.

In 2002 Pike sought to have her appeal legally stopped and to proceed with her execution. In June of that year Judge Leibowitz granted Pike's request and scheduled an execution date of 19 August 2002. However, a few days later Pike changed her mind and the Tennessee Court of Appeals subsequently stayed her execution. In October 2005, Pike's death sentence was affirmed; however, no execution date has been set at this time.

Pike was again in court in 2007 when her defense team headed by Donald E. Dawson asserted sought a new trial, alleging ineffective assistance of counsel in that her trial defense team failed to introduce evidence supporting Pike's alleged bipolar disorder. During this hearing, Shipp admitted to misinforming investigators and that he, in fact, was primarily responsible for Slemmer's murder. He stated that he was drunk and tired and just wanted the police to leave him alone when he put the onus of blame on Pike. Additional testimony from prior Job Corps student and the defendants' mutual friend Tyrone Comfort stated that Shipp controlled and abused Pike despite her assertions that he was the first male to protect her and she admired the respect and fear he elicited from others. Pike, however, was heavily medicated during this hearing for her alleged bipolar condition and the hearing was rescheduled for April 2008.

During her 2008 hearing, prosecutors portrayed Pike as a cold-blooded vicious killer who not only planned Slemmer's murder but prolonged it for sport, essentially playing cat-and-mouse with Slemmer by allowing her to get up and try to escape and then pushing her back on the ground for additional torture. Ultimately, her request for a new trial was denied.

Pike became newsworthy again in 2012 when she formulated an escape plan with the help of 34-year-old New Jersey resident Donald Kohut who frequently visited Pike in prison but the extent of their relationship remains unknown, and 23-year-old former prison guard Justin Heflin. In a joint investigation by the Tennessee Department of Corrections, the Tennessee Bureau of Investigation, and the New Jersey State Police after receiving information about the plan, both men were arrested and charged with bribery and conspiracy to commit escape, with Heflin charged with an additional facilitation to commit escape charge due to his job as a prison guard. Authorities discovered contraband evidence in the facility which could have only been brought in by a staff member and that Heflin was likely involved. Further investigation demonstrated that Heflin knew Kohut and that Heflin was receiving gifts and money for his assistance in the escape plan. Pike was also charged.

Even more recently, during yet another post-conviction relief hearing in 2015, testimony revealed that Pike was allegedly pregnant at the time of the murder. While this may be true it neither excuses her actions nor provides any potential evidence of legal insanity to justify an affirmative defense of not guilty by reason of mental disease or defect or guilty but mentally ill. Also during this hearing, Slemmer's mother requested the missing piece of her daughter's skull so she could bury the whole of her daughter but was denied as the skull piece remains a critical piece of evidence in Pike's ongoing legal appeals.

Since exhausting the state appeal process, Pike's new defense attorney, Assistant Federal Defender Stephen A. Ferrell, filed a

123-page petition on her behalf alleging that he constitutional rights were violated in both the original 1996 trial and penalty phase and that Tennessee's appellate courts ignored said violations. Among these claims is that capital punishment would amount to cruel and unusual punishment in violation of the Eighth Amendment of the United States Constitution because of Pike's youth, immaturity and mental illness. While Shipp—only 17 at the time of the murder—was too young to warrant imposition of a death sentence, Pike was not. Ferrell alleged that her trial lawyers were incompetent and failed to introduce evidence of mental illness, brain injury, and post-traumatic stress disorder. In response, the state Attorney General submitted a 90-page rebuttal repeatedly asserting that the state courts' ruling were all legally correct. As of the beginning of 2016, this battle continues.

Numerous video interviews of Pike over the past several years show her admitting that she was fully cognizant of her actions and that they were wrong. She stated that she felt as though she was taking out years of abuse on Slemmer and that she committed a horrible atrocity and deserves to be punished; however, she asserts that she deserves life without the possibility of parole for her actions; not the death penalty for the actions of three individuals. She has repeatedly stated that she wishes it was she who died and not Slemmer but such protestations are moot after the fact. One cannot help but wonder if Pike actually means what she says or is simply saying what she thinks others want to her. Knoxville Police Department detective Randy York who worked the case has said that in his lengthy career he has not encountered many people who he believes are evil but that Pike is, indeed, the personification of evil and that she should never be permitted to be around other human beings ever again.

Experts assert that the death penalty is not an effective general deterrent and debate over the morality and legality of capital punishment remains contentious and in the forefront of public discourse and debate. Currently, Tennessee is only one of 38 states which have the death penalty. Whereas women comprise 13% of those arrested for murder, only 2% are sentenced to death and, of those, only 3% are actually executed; primarily due to judges not wanting to sentence women to death. In Tennessee, only two individuals on death row have been executed—both males. The last time a woman was executed in the state was in 1837. Many currently believe that Pike will likely never be executed.

SHARON KINNEY : KILLER SLUT

DARLA POOLE

"Sharon Kinney didn't want to be a normal average American woman. And crime gave that to her." - FBI profile Candice DeLong

Sharon Kinne committed two murders in 1960, shooting her husband James Kinne as well as Patricia Jones, wife of her lover.

Initially, Sharon was not charged with the death of James Kinne as she laid the blame on her two-year-old daughter whom she said "like to play with her daddy's guns."

She was later tried for the murder of Patricia Jones several times, however, with each case ending in a mistrial. Sharon would then escape to Mexico before a fourth trial could be held.

While in Mexico with yet another boyfriend, Sharon would kill a Mexican radio announcer named Francisco Ordonez. She would not escape the hand of justice this go around as she would be convicted in a Mexican court of law and be sentenced to ten years in jail. Three more years additional years were added onto her sentence after she unsuccessfully appealed.

But Sharon would never take defeat lying down. She would escape from the Mexican prison in December of 1969 and would remain at large to this very day.

This is her story.

CHAPTER ONE – A LIFE OF QUIET DESPERATION

Sharon Elizabeth Hall was born on November 30th, 1939 to Doris and Eugene Hall. She was born and raised in the town of Independence, Missouri with a brief departure to the state of Washington during her junior high school years. Sharon returned to Missouri at the age of fifteen where she attended William Chrisman High school. Her early years were relatively uneventful as her father did construction work. Her upbringing was middle class and Sharon displayed no outward signs of anti-social behavior.

During a Mormon church function in the summer of 1956, sixteen-year-old Sharon met twenty-two-year-old college student

James Kinne. The two would begin dating until Kinne returned to his studies at Brigham Young University that fall.

Sharon wanted to find a man who would take her away from the drudgery of Independence. The two engaged in pre-marital relations with Sharon seducing James out of his restrictive religious beliefs. She would letter write a letter to James while he was away at school and inform him that she was pregnant.

James would leave his studies at BYU and return to Independence where he would "do the right thing" and marry Sharon.

The couple married in October of 1956 but the marriage was doomed from the start. The couple really didn't love each other. James simply gave into his lust while Sharon used him for a way out of her mundane life at home.

The sixteen-year-old Sharon listed herself as eighteen on the marriage license and as a widow. When asked about her widowhood, she told people that she had been married briefly while she lived in Washington but her husband died in a car accident.

The couple would have two weddings with their second being a church affair at the Mormon Tabernacle after Sharon had converted to accommodate James' Mormon beliefs.

After tying the knot, the couple moved to Provo, Utah where James could continue his studies at Brigham Young. At the end of the fall semester, however, James quit school. He returned to Independence with Sharon and they both entered the workforce.

Sharon earned money by babysitting and working in small shops. James found work as an electrical engineer at Bendix Aviation.

Sharon would claim to miscarry their first child but she soon became pregnant. In 1957, the couple would welcome their first child, Danna, into the world.

The young couple would have another child but by March of 1960, their marriage was on the rocks. Sharon did not earn that much money and had to spend time at home taking care of the children. James was the sole breadwinner and found his checks being eaten up by Sharon's spending habits.

Sharon was twenty years old and already wanting more out of life than James could provide. He was a small town boy who said "aw, shucks" a lot and began grate on the young wife's nerves.

James tried to appease his beautiful young wife who felt entitled to the best in life. James would rent out a home next door to his parents and then built a ranch-style home in Independence. He worked the night shift at Bendix while Sharon would spend her days shopping and hanging out with other men.

"James fell victim to his the idealism of the times," forensic psychologist Tim Newton said. "He thought that if he gave Sharon all of the stuff she wanted then she would come around and give him the respect he deserved. What he didn't realize was Sharon was a different kind of woman, definitely not the 1950s June Cleaver type. She had her own moral code. And that code was to serve herself at the cost of everyone around her."

CHAPTER TWO – WANTS AND DESIRES

"I want a new Thunderbird!" Sharon repeated her demand as a mantra whenever James would come home after a long night's work.

"No."

"Aren't you tired, James? Tired of driving the same dull car every day. Those new Thunderbirds are soooo luxurious. We need to buy one."

"We don't have the money," James said, before trudging off to bed.

Sharon quickly grew bored with the marriage and the children. She would have another child named Troy but continue to carry on with other men.

John Boldizs was one of those men. A friend of Sharon since high school, he appealed to Sharon's carnal desires but not her financial wants.

"Sharon grew a hatred for the restrictive lifestyle of James," Morgan said. "She did not like the Mormon attitudes toward life and women in particular. So the marriage started deteriorating fast as James could not satiate any of Sharon's desires. No one could."

James began seeing the writing on the wall. He grew tired of Sharon's unpredictable shopping sprees and became suspicious that she was cheating on him

On March 18th, 1960, he had informed his parents that he wanted out of the marriage.

"She's okay with the divorce," James said. "But she wants to keep the house and Danna. She also wants a $1,000."

His parents, devout Mormons, convinced James to stick with the marriage.

"His parents were blinded to the dark side of Sharon," Morgan said. "They came from a mindset that a woman could do no wrong. They did not see that side of Sharon. She could be cold and calculating but somehow go onto the good side of people. You couldn't help but like her because you know that she didn't give a damn what you thought."

The idea of murdering James for profit began to percolate in Sharon's mind. She jokingly offered John Boldizs a thousand dollars cash if he could "kill her husband or find someone who would."

On March 19th, a day after James would tell his parents he wanted to divorce Sharon, police were called to the Kinne home.

Inside, they found James lying on the bed with a bullet in his forehead.

Sharon would report hearing a gunshot coming from the bedroom where James was sleeping. When she went inside, she claimed she found the two-and-a-half-year-old Danna on the bed next to her father.

The young child was holding one of James' guns, a 22 caliber semi-automatic pistol.

Sharon then called for an ambulance but they pronounced him dead on arrival at the hospital.

"My two-year-old daughter was playing with the gun," Sharon said, mascara tears streaking down her face. "It was loaded and when the gun discharged it hit James in the head."

Police were not able to recover any fingerprints from the pistol and a paraffin test (gunshot residue) was not given to either Danna or Sharon. Family and neighbors came forward and testified that James had often let Danna play with the guns.

Police noted that the young girl had a familiarity with the pistol that belied her age. The two-year-old had the ability to unlatch the safety lever and point the gun. Satisfied that the death was an accident, they did not file any charges.

The gun was remanded to the police as evidence and never returned to Sharon. She lobbied regularly to get the gun back but the authorities refused her request.

Sharon would collect his life insurance, a whopping $29,000 ($232,000 in 2016 dollars).

"Sharon Kinne was a sociopath," forensic psychologist Candice Delong said. "She had no guilt. No remorse about hurting anyone. She had no empathy for human life other than her own."

CHAPTER THREE – THUNDERBIRDS AND BOY TOYS

Walter Jones was married to a woman named Patricia and had two children with his high school sweetheart. A former Marine, he moved to Independence five years earlier. Patricia worked for the IRS while Walter sold cars.

Walter loved the ladies and immediately fell for Sharon the moment she stepped on his lot. With the insurance money in hand, Sharon finally had the opportunity to buy her dream car, a Ford Thunderbird. The two began an affair and Sharon looked upon the confident Walter as marriage material.

Sharon asked Walter to accompany her on a trip to Washington that May but the married man refused. She went on the trip anyway and when she returned, she used the same trick she used on James to get the man she wanted to commit.

"I'm pregnant," she said.

"What?" Walter asked, hearing her but not believing it.

"I'm pregnant," Sharon repeated. "And you're the father."

"We have to end this," Walter said, his face turning red.

"What?"

"You. Me. Us. It's over."

Sharon became enraged at Walter's attitude, fully expecting the car salesman to leave his wife for her.

"I told her to wait and see what happened," Walter testified at one of Sharon's trials. "I told her it was all over between us."

"Naked and screaming, Sharon followed Walter's car into the street, cursing and threatening to get even with him, as neighbors watched carrying-ons of a woman who had lost her husband less than three months earlier," a local newspaper reported.

The married car salesman had no idea the kind of psychopath Sharon was. Sharon would not let go and had to settle the score. She contacted Patricia at her IRS office of employment and informed her that Walter was having an affair with her sister. Sharon offered to meet Patricia at an undisclosed location where she meant to rat out the man that refused her hand in marriage.

Patricia would meet Sharon at the ended of a wooded street, a place known as a lover's lane for young romantics.

Sharon would pull a gun on Patricia and fire four shots in the form of a cross into the unsuspecting woman.

With his wife not returning home, Walter Jones filed a missing person report with the police the next day. He made frantic calls to neighbors and family asking if they had seen Patricia.

Her co-workers reported that Patricia had, in fact, received a call that day from an unknown woman who wanted to meet with her.

Patricia left work as usual with her carpool partners and asked to be dropped off on a street corner in Independence.

Patricia's car pool friends saw a woman waiting for her but did not recognize her as someone they knew.

His worst fears becoming realized, Walter called Sharon and asked if she had met with his wife. Sharon admitted to seeing Patricia and was going to tell her about their affair. Sharon went on to say that she saw Patricia talking to a man in a green 1957 Ford.

Walter became angry and went to Sharon's home.

The six-foot, two-hundred pound Marine was not to be trifled with. He held a knife to the Sharon's throat, threatening to cut her if she didn't tell him more.

Sharon talked her way out of the bad situation, convincing Walter that she did not know what happened to Patricia.

CHAPTER FOUR – DEAD WOMAN IN A DITCH

Sharon would call "Johnnie" Boldizs, her old standby boyfriend, and told him that she was worried that her friend was missing. She suggested they might find Patricia parked with someone on one of the many lover's lane roads around the town. Boldizs refused to "snoop" but agreed to accompany Sharon if they could visit one of the lover's lane themselves.

Ever the horn dog, Boldizs drove out with Sharon to their old make-out spot on Phelps Road in Independence, MO.

Getting out of the car, Sharon had "discovered" the body of Patricia in a wooded area.

"Let's get out of here and call the cops," Boldiz insisted.

"Well, take me home first," Sharon said. "Don't implicate me because I'm probably the last one who saw her alive."

Patricia had been shot four times with a .22 caliber pistol. She had a fatal wound to her head, the bullet had entered through her mouth on an upward trajectory. She also had a bullet that went through her stomach and two shots to her shoulders that came through on a downward trajectory. There were powder burns on the hemline of her skirt and police surmised that she had been killed at close rage.

"I was helping him look for his wife," Sharon said to the police. "He thought she was going out to meet another man. This street ends in a secluded lover's lane. We wanted to catch her in the act. Instead, we found her dead."

Police interrogated Sharon, Walter Jones, and James Bondizs. Jones and Boldizs both admitted to having sexual relations with Sharon and agreed to take lie detector tests which they both would pass. Sharon gave an oral statement but refused to sign a written statement or take a lie detector test.

Police had little luck obtaining evidence at the crime scene. They sifted the dirt trying to find the bullet that passed through Patricia's stomach. They employed a troop of Boy Scouts to help search for the gun in the area. This proved to be unsuccessful as did the dragging of a nearby body of water in the hopes of finding the weapon.

A .22 caliber rifle slug was found buried in the dirt where Jones' body had been discovered and police were satisfied that the killing had most likely taken place where the body was found.

Sharon would be arrested at her home for Patricia's murder a few days later. Jackson County Sheriffs also took the opportunity to arrest her for the death of James Kinne as well. She was later released on a $20,000 bond while she awaited her first hearing.

CHAPTER FIVE – COVERING HER TRACKS

Patricia Jones had been shot with a .22 caliber pistol and investigators discovered that Sharon had recently purchased the same type of gun. She convinced a male co-worker to purchase the gun for her but ordered him not to register the gun in her name.

Police searched her home for the gun in question and found nothing although they did find a box which they believed once contained the weapon.

"I lost that gun," Sharon said when questioned. "Lost it when I took a trip to Washington."

When interrogated about the gun later she stated that the weapon "just disappeared."

Her paramour Walter Jones did not get off Scott-free either. Police arrested him as a material witness in the case but he posted a $2,000 bond and was released.

Sharon would be arraigned on July 11th and was initially denied bail. She would eventually be freed on a $24,000 bond. At this time, she was three months pregnant and would give birth to a daughter named Maria Christine on January 16th, 1961.

Sharon would stand for the murder of Patricia in June of 1961. The all-male jury heard arguments which centered around cases built on differing times of death. The prosecution would state that Patricia had died more than 24 hours before Sharon found her body while the defense would claim the death occurred six to eight hours before.

The chief witness for the prosecution was Detective Harry Nesbitt who stated that Sharon had told him that she was afraid Walter was drifting away from her. She offered Walter financial support and tried to reel him in with the fact that she was pregnant with his child. The prosecution failed, however, in establishing the fact that Sharon owned or was in the possession of the gun that killed Patricia.

The jury deliberated for only ninety minutes. They found Sharon not guilty because of "just too many loopholes" with the prosecution's case.

Sharon had acquired celebrity status for the crime and one of the jurors, Ogden Stephens, asked Sharon for her autograph and she happily obliged.

But the police smelled blood. After she was acquitted, authorities immediately arrested her for the murder of her husband James.

They no longer believed that the two-year-old pulled the trigger during an "accident." Police hired a gun expert for the trial who testified that a child of that age would not have been able to pull the trigger on the gun that blew off James Kinne's head.

CHAPTER SIX – TRY AND TRY AGAIN

In the first trial for her husband's murder, the district attorney did not want the death penalty for Sharon. The prosecution also focused primarily on the testimony of Sharon's lover, John Boldizs. He would retract on his claim that Sharon offered him $1,000 to kill her husband.

"It was approximately two weeks to four weeks before Kinne's death," Boldizs said. "We was talking about her husband. She said, 'Would you kill my husband for $1,000?' I said, 'No. Hell no.' She said, 'Do you know of anybody that would?' I said 'Yes; I know somebody.' She said, 'If you find somebody, let me know.' I said, 'Yes.' But I never did."

"Do you have a feeling she was serious in her request?" the prosecutor asked.

"I believe so, now. She said 'Well, I'll just give you a grand. You can bump off my old man. Then I said, 'No, man. Like we wouldn't do that.'"

"Did you think it was a joke," Sharon's defense attorney asked, pressing the issue.

"It was just like if I'd say to you, 'I'd give you $100 to jump off city hall,'" Boldizs said.

Sharon's defense team immediately attacked the testimony of John Boldiz. "He was a poor mixed up kid who would sign anything," they argued. They also presented the argument that the young Danna had been able to pull triggers on toy guns with stiffer pulls than the .22 caliber used to kill her father.

The prosecuting attorney, J. Arnot Hill, remained steadfast in his closing argument as he believed that Sharon was truly serious about giving Boldizs a grand to kill her husband.

Sharon's defense attorney used their closing argument to soften the judgment of her promiscuous behavior. "It is not your role to judge her for being loose. What ever breach of the moral law, she has suffered and her God will chastise her. She has done plenty of penance for that."

The jury would deliberate for five and a half hours. They would convict Sharon of first-degree murder which Sharon met with stoic acceptance.

The judge sentenced her to life in prison at the Missouri Reformatory for Women.

Amazingly, James Kinne's family continued in their support of their murderous daughter-in-law, believing her to be innocent.

"We can't find it in our hearts to say anything bad about her," Kinne's parents said in a statement to the press. "We still don't feel that she committed murder."

"The verdict was a mistake," Sharon said afterward.

Her attorney's would eventually appeal to the Missouri Supreme Court which would reverse Sharon's convictions in March of 1963. They ordered a new trial because Sharon's defense had been denied peremptory challenges during jury selection.

Sharon would be denied bail initially but that decision would be overturned in July of 1963 as her brother would post $25,000 bond.

Sharon would then take her children and move in with her mother before the new trial began.

CHAPTER SEVEN – A BROKEN SYSTEM

Sharon's second trial would begin on March 23rd, 1964. The jury selection process would last over fourteen hours. Presiding judge Paul Carver had to sequester the jury due to the notoriety of the case. A mistrial would be declared when it was discovered that a law partner of the prosecuting attorney had once been retained by one of the jurors.

A third trial was then scheduled for June 29th, 1964. Once again, the jury selection process was a grueling one, lasting more than twelve hours. The testimony of her boyfriend John Boldiz remained the same, he once again stated that Sharon jokingly offered him $1,000 to kill her husband. But he further revealed that Sharon had told him not to tell police about the offer. A female acquaintance of Sharon took the stand this time around and testified that Sharon had joked that she should "get rid of your old man like I did."

The prosecution would reveal what later became known as the "Precious Tomcat" letters. These were letters that Sharon had written to her cell mate lover, Margaret Hopkins. Hopkins was an older woman she met in prison. Sharon had quickly learned the ropes in prison, obtaining an older lesbian lover for protection.

Sharon had entered into a handwritten "marriage contract" with Margaret during their time in prison together. Margaret would be released from jail prior to Sharon. In one of the letters, Sharon instructed Margaret to go to her grandmother's home and get the .22 caliber gun. The letter stated that the gun was hidden in a wall by the chimney.

"Lies!" Sharon would shot from her defense table. "All lies!"

Police would search the home of Sharon's grandmother but would later discover that she had moved. They ended up searching the wrong house.

No gun. No evidence.

Sharon would then take the stand on the last day of the trial. Looking somber yet elegant in a tight black dress, she addressed the all-male jury with her story of what place the night her husband James was killed.

"He had just cleaned his .22 and left it on the pillow beside him while he took a nap," Sharon said. "We were supposed to attend a church function and I was getting ready in the bathroom."

"Danna came into the bathroom trying to get me to play with her. She made several trips to the bedroom trying to get attention from James. She brought in several toys and asked him questions. Then I heard Danna in the bedroom. She was saying 'Show me this, Daddy. Show me this.' just as she had done several times before with her toys. And I heard a shot, I guess it was a shot. I went into the bedroom and Danna was standing there and James was lying there and I saw the blood and I thought he was dead. I picked up Danna and put her on the couch and called James's father."

She charmed enough of the all-male jury, deadlocking them seven-to-five in favor of acquittal.

This would result in a mistrial.

CHAPTER EIGHT – FOURTH TIME AIN'T NO CHARM

A fourth trial was scheduled for October 1964 but this go around Sharon would not put her life in the hands of the system. By this time, her mother had moved in with her and ran interference to

any authorities and press that came around.

Sharon then plotted her own escape. She became a barfly at the many low rent Mafia bars in her town, sleeping around with as many men as she could. It was in one of these bars that she met Sal Puglise, a petty thief and con artist. The two quickly became lovers and signed a handwritten "marriage contract" just like the one had signed with her cell-block lover, Margaret Hopkins.

Knowing that she would not be returning to Independence anytime soon, Sharon passed a series of bad checks around town. She didn't want to drop any more money than she had to.

In September of 1964, she was still free on bond. She took a vacation in Mexico with her new lover, Sal Puglise. She left her children with James Kinne's father while traveling under the name of "Jeanette Puglise", making as if she were Puglise's wife.

The couple had arrived in Mexico to get married. The terms of her bail permitted her to leave the country but the company that performed the bail required that she receive written permission from them in order to travel.

Sharon got around that loophole by using the fake name as she crossed the border. Sharon said she felt unsafe traveling in the foreign country and bought another gun in Mexico in addition to the one she had brought with her.

On the night of September 18th, 1964, Sharon left the hotel alone after an argument with Puglise. It is unclear whether she went to get money or get medication that she needed. Puglise would later claim that they were in their hotel room when Sharon complained of feeling faint. She wanted him to go out and get some medicine for her but he refused. Instead, she left by herself. She walked to the Del Prado Hotel but found the pharmacy closed. From there she went to a shady-looking hotel bar and asked for a drink of water.

An English speaking man offered to buy her a drink and she accepted. His name was Francisco Parades Ordonez. He was a Mexican-born American citizen who worked as a radio announcer in Chicago. He quickly became smitten with the beauty of Sharon and began plying her with drinks.

Sharon then stated that Ordonez invited her back to his room to show her some photographs and where she could rest as she claimed that she "wasn't feeling well."

"I lay down," Sharon recalled. "He took off his jacket and got me a glass of water. After a while, I started to feel better and told Mr. Paredes that I was leaving. He made some advances. When I pushed him away, he hit me and then put his knee on my stomach. He hit me several times. He covered my mouth so I could not scream, but I managed to throw him off and onto the floor. It gave me time to pull my gun from my purse. I fired — I don't know how many times; one or two."

Sharon insisted that she didn't want to kill or harm Ordonez. She only wanted to scare him but her bullets hit him in the chest, killing him.

The hotel manager, Enrique Martinez Rueda entered the room upon hearing the gunfire.

Bursting through the door, he saw Ordonez laying on the floor with two bullets in his chest.

Sharon stood over the dead man, smoking gun in hand, and then shot the hotel manager in the shoulder.

There are two competing stories as to what happened next. One story tells of Rueda having the presence of mind to run out of the room and lock Sharon inside. The other is Sharon getting into her car and heading for the gates but Rueda locked the gates in time and does not let her leave until the police arrive.

CHAPTER NINE – MEXICAN JUSTICE

The Mexican police believed that Sharon went out that evening to rob someone and had chosen Ordonez. When the man refused her demands, she shot him.

Mexican authorities searched Sharon's room at the Hotel Gin where they found two more guns and a supply of shells. They then searched through her purse, finding another gun and fifty bullets.

Her boyfriend, Puglise, would be taken into custody as well. They held him on the charge of entering Mexico illegally and carrying an unlicensed gun.

The couple would be held in separate prisons for their respective trials.

Puglise would be declared innocent of the charges brought against him and would be sent back to the United States.

But Sharon would find Mexican juries to be not as friendly as those in America.

"I just don't think about it," Sharon said before her sentencing for the Ordonez murder. "If I did I might be miserable, but I just refuse to look at things that way. I haven't given up hope and I don't think I ever will."

She remained resigned to the fact that she would receive some type of sentencing. "They (Mexican authorities) wouldn't feel they have done their duty unless they give me at least a few years in jail here."

Reporters commented that she seemed more worried about forfeiting a bond than the actual sentencing. "I could always use the money," Sharon said. "I don't intend to spend all my life in jail."

Her words later prove to be prophetic.

CHAPTER TEN – LA PISTOLERA

Authorities in Kansas would obtain the gun found in the couple's hotel room. Ballistic tests would reveal that the gun matched the weapon used to kill Patricia Jones in 1960. American authorities did not bother with extradition as they could not try Sharon again for the same crime.

The Mexican jury would find her guilty, however, and Sharon would be sentenced to ten years in prison. She again tried to appeal but that failed and resulted in three more years being added to her sentence.

Her fellow prisoners would refer to her as "La Pistolera" (female gunslinger) and the Mexican media followed suit, headlining their stories about her with that nickname.

Sharon would appeal as she did in the United States but her efforts would result in an increased sentence as the Mexican judge thought her initial sentencing to be "too lenient."

Now instead of serving ten years she was serving thirteen.

Sharon would remain in the Mexican prison system for over five years until December 7th, 1969. She would not present for a routine roll call at the Ixtapalapan jail. The prison guards were so slack that Sharon would not be declared an escapee until after she failed to show up at a second roll-call later that evening.

Her escape would not be reported to Mexican police until hours later as the jail staff tried to locate her on the prison grounds, believing she may be hiding somewhere.

A manhunt ensued and authorities focused on the northern region of Mexico. Investigators believed that Sharon could be heading toward the home of a former inmate that she befriended while in jail.

The FBI was alerted by Mexican authorities but agents did not think Sharon would attempt to return to the United States.

Multiple theories abound as to how she escaped and if she escaped at all. One theory is that Sharon bribed guards to look the other way while she made her escape out of the prison. A blackout had occurred the evening of her disappearance and it was later discovered that a door that should have been locked had been left unsecured. Another theory posited that Sharon used her feminine wiles to enlist the aid of a Mexico City policeman who was her boyfriend at the time. A more sinister theory speculates that the family of Francisco Parades Ordonez had helped her escape then promptly killed her.

The search for Sharon lasted only twelve days. Police believed that Sharon had crossed the border from Mexico into Guatemala which would negate their entire investigation.

Sharon was fluent in Spanish after the five years in the Mexican jail and could easily blend in no matter where she wound up.

By the end of December of 1969, Sharon was ostensibly a free woman with no law enforcement authority actively engaged in finding her whereabouts.

"That's quite a feat," Delong said. "And she pulled it off. That's the kind of person she was. Nothing could stand in her way. Not even prison."

To this day, Sharon Kinne has not been found.

Bonus story : Joan Shannon

Chapter 1: In the Beginning

David Shannon was an ordinary, down-to-earth, American man. When he was just six years old David told his mother he was going to join the army one day, and thirteen years later David achieved this lifelong goal when he enlisted at the age of nineteen.

After saying goodbye to his family, David moved from his hometown Langdon, North Dakota, to upstate New York where he was newly stationed. It was here that he met Joan, a single mother of two who worked in a topless bar. Joan quickly captured David's heart, and David Joan's. This was clear when Joan proposed to David only a year after they met. David was unlike anyone Joan had ever met, he was willing to protect and care for Joan and her two daughters without trying to control her. He was sweet and funny, and Joan didn't want anyone else to have the chance to figure out how great of a man he was.

But Joan had a very different past than David—they came from separate worlds. While David grew up in a loving household, Joan's childhood was characterized by her being sexually assaulted at twelve years old, and her being abandoned by both her parents shortly after. When Joan was only eighteen, she wound up married to an abusive husband who she had two daughters with in quick succession.

Later, after David and Joan were married in a small North Dakota church, David adopted these two daughters, Daisy and Elizabeth, and loved them as his own, just as he did his own two sons that Joan later bore him. He loved them because he loved Joan. It was as simple as that for him. This love was altogether ripped from his grasp in 2002 though when he was fatally shot twice while he slept in his bed one rainy July night.

Chapter 2: Fayetteville

David was well-suited to serving in the military. He became a well-respected serviceman and was quickly promoted to the rank of Major, working for Special Operations in a field that required him to use his computer whizz skills. In the year 2000, the major was transferred to Fort Bragg, an army base located in Fayetteville, North Carolina. It would be here, smack-dab in the middle of the bible belt, that the couple's secret sins would catch up with them.

It was no surprise to anyone that the Shannons ended up in Fayetteville. Three-time winner of the All-America City Award from the National Civic League, Fayetteville was well-known for being a military town. Both the Pope Army Airfield and the Fort Bragg military base, home of the Special Operations Forces, called Fayetteville home. In the past, Fort Bragg had been the home of the Field Artillery at the onset of World War II, housing all the Army's artillery units east of the Mississippi River. It also became an important station during the Vietnam War when it became the housing station for the Army's 9th Infantry Division. David, now well on his way to becoming a Colonel, fit right in.

While Fort Bragg continues to be a respected military base well into the 21st Century, in the 90's the military base became synonymous with something that had nothing to do with respect: murder.

Chapter 3: Fort Bragg Murders

Fort Bragg had been the setting of several murders in the past—all involving army husbands murdering their families. This string of murders caused the military to open an investigation about the stresses the army was placing on its men and how this could have contributed to these tragedies. Ultimately, this investigation led to a number of recommendations, all of which were followed through with varying degrees of commitment.

The murders themselves were all gruesome. The earliest occurred on February 17, 1970. Jeffrey R. MacDonald, a Special Forces Green Beret stationed at Fort Bragg, murdered his pregnant wife and two daughters aged five and two at the time. MacDonald denied responsibility for the crimes, blaming instead a dangerous cult, but was ultimately convicted of the crime.

Later, in 1985, Timothy Hennis, a master sergeant raped and murdered his wife before slicing the throats of two of his daughters, aged five and three at the time. Hennis' case caught a lot of attention in the media as he was awaited his trial on death row for two years before having his conviction overturned. In a second trial, Hennis was acquitted of the crime altogether. It wasn't until 2010 that a cold case team was ultimately able to prove his guilt beyond a reasonable doubt.

In 2002, months before David Shannon's murder, all hell broke loose for Fort Bragg when four wives were killed by their husbands in six weeks. In all four cases, the husband was found guilty of the crime. All four husbands had also recently returned from a special operations mission in Afghanistan. It would be these four murders that led to the military's investigations into the stress deployment has on our nation's families.

Chapter 4: David's Murder

While David's murdered occurred in his home just blocks from the Fort Bragg base, it was anything but similar to the rest of the Fort Bragg murders. For a start, the rest of the murders were at the hands of the husbands, in David's case, the husband was the victim.

On July 22, 2002, David was murdered while he slept next to his wife Joan in his family house. The shooter had entered the room, pointed the gun directly at David's head, and pulled the trigger. Shortly after this first shot rang out, the gun was placed against his chest and fired again. Joan later stated that she did not hear the first shot, but was conscious when the second one was fired. She was unable to describe the intruder, stating to police that she only saw a shadow—an indication of movement—in the dark room.

After waking to the unforgettable sight of her husband's brains splattered on their bedroom walls, Joan immediately ran down the hall to make sure her children were safe. The night their father was murdered, three out of four of the Shannon children were in the house. While their oldest daughter, Daisy, was out of town, both of their sons aged seven and ten at the time were present, as well as Elizabeth and her best friend Vera who had slept over that night. After establishing no one else in the home had been harmed, Joan placed a frantic 911 call that caused the immediate response of paramedics and police officers. David was pronounced dead by the first responders to the scene.

Chapter 5: The first signs

First responders still recall the bad feeling they had when they arrived at the Shannon household that July night. For starters, Joan, who had been hysterical on the 911 call, was now oddly calm. Joan was recounting the experience like a well-rehearsed story and had also somehow managed to escape the scene with little to no blood on herself—a clear sign she had made no attempt to hold or provide assistance to David after the attack. When police officers confirmed to Joan that David had died, Joan asked them specifically to break the news to Elizabeth.

Police officers complied, telling the fifteen-year-old girl that her stepfather, who had raised her as his own, had been shot twice. Elizabeth's only reply was the simple question: "did he die?"

These oddities were fresh in the minds of police officers when they began their investigation in the Shannon household.

Police began the investigation into David Shannon's murder the same night it happened, but it was off to a rough start. Besides the odd behavior of David's wife and his step-daughter Elizabeth, investigators had little to go on. Soon after entering the house they realized that gathering physical evidence was going to be next to impossible as the house was in an extreme state of disarray. There was garbage all over the place, and it looked like no laundry or clothing had been cleaned in weeks. Despite the mess, police were able to quickly rule out certain common motives such as robbery, as nothing was taken, and any violence or sexually driven motives as no one else was harmed.

It was clear that the attack on the Shannon house that night was meant for David and David only.

Because of David's high-ranking and highly-secretive position in the military, investigators naturally figured that David's killer may have been related to David's work. However, nothing really came of this. Police were faced with frequent and abrupt dead ends every time they tried to persuade a new lead connected to the army. However, once police began to search deeper into the Shannon household, they made a startling discovery that flipped the entire investigation on its heels.

In David and Shannon's bedroom closet was a massive amount of pornography and sex toys.

Chapter 6: Joan and the Swingers

The discovery of a hoard of pornographic material and sex toys in an area so accessible to the house's children immediately shattered the wholesome family image investigators had of the Shannons. No one who cares about their children keeps thousands of photos of themselves having sex with strangers somewhere where the children could quite easily stumble upon them.

The discovery of this material also changed the course of the investigation in another dramatic way. When Joan was asked why this material, which included an uncountable number of photos of herself having sex with other men—sometimes more than one at a time—existed, Joan was happy to share the answer with the officers. It was simple, she said, she and David were swingers—they participated in recreational sex parties where the couple would sleep with other people.

After learning this, investigators were almost certain that whoever killed David was familiar with Joan. They now just needed to figure out how.

Swinging was important in Joan and David's relationship. Joan had an insatiable appetite for sex and needed more than what David could give her. Coincidentally, David was a voyeurist—he liked to watch his wife have sex with other people. They were a match made in hell. Joan would feed her sexual appetite with as many men as she could get her hands on, and David would take hundreds of souvenir photos and find his own pleasure in watching.

Joan and David participated in swinging for the majority of their eleven-year marriage. They started during their time in upstate New York, where Joan claims they attended regular swinging parties. This habit continued after moving to Fayetteville where it was David who made the first contact with other swinging couples via the internet within a month after moving to the Bible belt city.

Chapter 8: Elizabeth

Swinging, especially to the extent that Joan and David were involved, is a time commitment. It requires a lot of a person's time, energy, and emotions. In order to accommodate all these things, a person can't continue to live a regular life on the side—if swinging becomes your priority, the rest of your life gets left behind. And this, unfortunately, seemed to be the case with Joan.

Joan loved swinging. She loved the attention and the physical pleasure. It was an addiction. But like any addiction, it had a negative impact in other areas of her life. For Joan, her family got left behind as she pursued the affections of others.

Joan and David's children once stated to police that they could not remember a time during their childhood where they felt loved by their parents—especially their mother. Joan was too selfish to pay her children much attention and she didn't seem to demand any instructional control over them. All discipline was left in the hands of David, the strict army man, who also had limited time in his swinging schedule leftover for his children. While this had a negative impact on all the children—the disgusting state of the household alone proved this for investigators—fifteen-year-old Elizabeth seemed to take the lack of attention the hardest.

Elizabeth was the typical rebellious child. She would stay out late with boys, take drugs, and always managed to sneak out of the house even after alarms were secured on her bedroom doors and windows.

Elizabeth was known for her short temper and how she would punish those who angered her by breaking their possessions. She got in fights, she skipped school, and she hated David.

Joan herself states that she simply gave up on trying to parent Elizabeth—the fifteen-year-old was out of control and Joan did not have the tools to rein her in. David tried his best to discipline Elizabeth, but their relationship had always been strained. Elizabeth, who already did not like authority figures, never accepted the Major as her father. She knew he wasn't her real dad and to her this meant that he should have no say in her life.

Elizabeth and her older sister Daisy were also suspicious about what their parents got up to in the house when they would all get sent away for the weekend and upon their return, their bedroom furniture had been rearranged. Although they didn't know the extent of it, they had a pretty good idea that their parents had a secretive hobby. One that was too X-Rated for them to be around.

Chapter 9: Jeff

Elizabeth and Daisy were not in the least bit wrong. Joan and David had grown involved with one swinger sex club in particular. The couples in this club would meet up monthly at a local hotel where they would swap partners for the night. The hotel would be set up in two separate rooms—one for meeting and greeting, the other for sex. During these get-togethers, there would be people having sex together right in front of one another. It was all casual. Members would propose sexual acts to one another, if the request was accepted they would engage in whatever sexual act they fancied, and after they would casually continue to drink with the group and chat. Sex, to these types of clubs, is a matter of fact. It's all about exploring your sexual fantasies with your spouse present. In the case of the Shannons, Joan had a very specific sexual fantasy she liked to fulfill as often as possible, and David knew it.

Joan liked to have sex with black men—something David was not able to provide her. But in the spirit of a true swinging partner, David went on the internet and found Joan a partner able to please her innermost desires. This partner was a fellow army member named Jeff.

Jeff was an average looking black man in his 30's. He was certainly not Denzel Washington, but he was far from unattractive. And, most importantly to the Shannons, he was open to the idea of swinging. When David asked Jeff if he would have sex with his wife, Jeff agreed. The two men then made tentative plans to meet at the next local swingers party.

Jeff was incredibly welcome at the sex club the Shannons attended—black men, to them, were a rare treat. And to Joan, having Jeff specially selected for her by David made him even more tantalizing. The first night they met, Joan and Jeff ended up engaging in several sexual acts, often with other members joining them, all while David watched from the corner of the room. It was an intense night of sexual fulfillment and fantasies come true for Joan. But as history shows, great passion is often followed by horrifying consequences.

A month after the first swingers party, Joan, Jeff, and David met again, this time with another one of Joan's specific fantasies in mind: gangbang swinging. For hours at that party, Joan had sex with multiple males, as much as four men at the same time, including both David and Jeff. The majority of explicit photos found by investigators on the Shannon's computer were from this particular night. It was an unforgettable evening.

After this party, however, something began to change between Joan and David for the worst. Although the couple returned home together, as usual, Joan seemed to leave a piece of herself with Jeff as well.

Joan couldn't stop thinking about Jeff. He stood out from all the other sexual romps she had participated in in the past. The two began to meet privately for sex. This change of scene made the sex more intimate for both Joan and Jeff. There was no one else there participating, watching—it was just the two of them locked in the passion of the moment.

Initially, the two began meeting once or twice a week for sex, but this quickly escalated to three or four. They almost couldn't keep their hands off one another. On top of this, Joan decided to not tell David about these meetings. She was breaking all the rules her and David had, lines were being blurred and soon Joan found herself crossing into the dangerous waters of an affair. But she couldn't help herself. The more Joan and Jeff would meet, the closer they became. Soon, the new couple began spending time together outside of the bedroom, they developed a close and intimate friendship. Joan felt close enough to Jeff that she would even bring him over to her family home and introduce him to her daughters as her new boyfriend. She was no longer interested in Jeff for the exoticism and pleasure he afforded her alone—she was now emotionally attached.

Chapter 10: Tension

While Joan never explicitly told David about her new relationship with Jeff, David could tell something had changed between the two of them. Joan had started to drift away from David, she no longer wanted to let him in emotionally and the couple was no longer having sex. On a hunch, David decided to call out Joan for these sudden changes. He told her that she needed to break off any relationships she was having outside their marriage.

As expected, this made Joan irate. One of the things she always loved about David was that he never tried to control or restrict her actions or desires, it was one of the reasons they clicked as a couple. And now he was doing just that. She told Jeff about this conversation and that she would not bend to David's will. Nothing would change between the new lovers.

Jeff and David also exchanged words about the subject over an online chat. To see if Joan was telling the truth about David's suspicions, Jeff reached out to David and asked him when the next time the married couple would be attending a party. David promptly replied that he and Joan were taking a break from the swinging lifestyle in order to work on their marriage, adding that Jeff was not to see Joan again. What began as David helping his wife fulfill all her sexual desires had quickly become a threesome of anger, jealousy, and lust. A deadly combination.

At the beginning of the Summer of 2002, Shannon clearly no longer wanted to continue her marriage with David; she now only saw her army Major husband as a roadblock between her and her idealistic future with Jeff, whom she was now madly in love with. Joan became so comfortable with this idea that she had no problem expressing this to her own daughters.

Unfortunately for Joan, divorce can be an expensive undertaking, especially when there are four children involved. This was money that Joan didn't have. She was stuck so close yet so far away from the only thing she now desired in the world—a future with Jeff.

Chapter 11: A Motive and a Method

Money can always be found when needed, however. And when Joan did some research, she found a jackpot just sitting at the tips of her fingers. Where? In life insurance policies.

Joan was the sole benefactor of a life insurance policy David had, which meant she stood to earn just shy of $800,000 in the event of David's sudden death. As a bonus, if David were to die, Joan also wouldn't have to fund a nasty divorce. It was the perfect solution in Joan's mind, and she wasn't shy to share this view. Several people close to Joan, including her own children, later told police that they had heard Joan say her life would be much easier if David were to die.

All Joan needed now was a plan.

Luckily for Joan, there was someone else in the house who shared her disdain for David—her troubled daughter Elizabeth. Elizabeth had had ill will towards David for years due to the fact that he was the only disciplinary figure in her life. She was not used to that type of attention and could not see that it came from a place of caring. David disciplined his step-daughter because he cared for her. He did not want her running with dangerous crowds and taking drugs. He wanted her to have a bright future. These sentiments were ultimately lost on Elizabeth who hated David a little bit more with each restriction he placed on her.

Elizabeth, however, also had a lot of disdain towards her mother, Joan. Elizabeth did not believe her mother ever loved her. She was too selfish for that. With her head wrapped around sex, love, and secrets, she had no time to think about Elizabeth. To make matters worse, Joan started bringing Jeff around the house more frequently. The last thing Elizabeth wanted was a second man around the house, and it insulted Elizabeth that she had to deal with David still when it was clear that even Joan no longer loved him.

At the start of the summer, Joan's neglect for her children came to a startling hault. Joan began doting on Elizabeth. They started spending time together at Joan's request. They would go shopping, to restaurants, and to movies, and Joan began buying Elizabeth everything she wanted. Elizabeth was blindsided by this sudden rush of affection but chose not to question it as she finally had the mother daughter relationship she had always wanted.

This became a very important time in Elizabeth's life, she became incredibly vulnerable as she tried to do everything she could to preserve this new thing in her life. She had crawled through a barren desert of loneliness and was not ready to leave the oasis quite yet.

Joan understood the new position she had with Elizabeth. She was no longer just her mother, she now had complete control over the young girl's thoughts and actions. She began speaking to Elizabeth on a daily basis about how it was David who did not want her to spend any time with her daughters. He did not approve of Joan paying more attention to her than him, he did not want Joan to spend money on Elizabeth—he was ruining their lives. When Elizabeth didn't want to hear it or stepped out of her new submissive role, Joan would punish her by withdrawing her love, leaving Elizabeth to beg and earn her attention back. It was a cocktail of chaos just ready to spill over and ruin the carpets.

Joan had created a strong ally in Elizabeth—she now hated her stepfather more than ever and felt a burning desire to do whatever would please her mother. As the two continued to spend time together, Joan slowly changed the narrative of how horrible their lives were with David, to what they could do to make things better. And to Joan, and now Elizabeth as well, there was only one real solution—David needed to die.

So Joan began plotting, and one day when the mood was just right, she popped the question she'd been waiting to ask for so long—Elizabeth, will you kill your step dad for me?

At first, Elizabeth said no. She didn't care how perfect a plan her mom had thought she had devised. Even though she wasn't overly fond of the guy, she did not want to kill the only person she had ever known to be her father. But Joan is not the type of person to take no for an answer.

Chapter 12: The Plan

Joan spent weeks wearing down Elizabeth's resolve. She played her old tricks of withdrawing her love and attention as well as a couple new tricks—begging and lying. Joan began asking Elizabeth to kill David several times a day. She hoped that eventually Elizabeth would grow tired of being asked and would cave. On top of this, Joan spent every spare minute of her day convincing Elizabeth that nothing would happen to her because of her age. They weren't going to send some misguided fifteen-year-old to prison. She would be absolutely fine. And besides, Joan had developed a foolproof plan that would allow Elizabeth to escape accusations in the first place.

Joan's plan was simple. David had multiple guns laying around the house that he did not pay a lot of attention to. It would be simple for Joan to take one of these guns without detection from the Army Major. Elizabeth would take this gun, practice shooting it a few times, and then would shoot her stepfather in the middle of the night. After shooting David, Elizabeth would ditch the gun and go back to bed while Joan called the police. They would simply play the attack off as a robbery gone wrong and Joan and Elizabeth would be free to spend the rest of their lives as the perfect mother and daughter all while the police searched for an intruder that didn't really exist. After a few years of no new leads, they would declare the case cold and all would be well.

After being pressured for weeks by the mother whose affections she had always wanted, Elizabeth eventually bent to Joan's will—she finally agreed to kill her own father.

Chapter 13: The Murder

Although Elizabeth had agreed to murder David, she and Joan had not set an official date. July 22, 2002, two days after Joan's latest sex romp with Jeff, Joan decided she could not spend another night married to David. Despite the fact that Elizabeth's best friend Vera was staying over at their house, Joan told Elizabeth that she must commit the murder that night.

Elizabeth had the gun and knew how to use it. She had practiced shooting the weapon the day before, again with Vera present. It was now or never. Joan went over the plan with Elizabeth again and gave her a pair of latex gloves and sent her on her own. David and Joan spent the evening watching a movie and went to bed together while their two sons slept down the hall. Elizabeth and Vera spent their night doing the typical sleepover routine for young girls. They sat in Elizabeth's room and chatted about boys while listening to music. Eventually, Vera fell asleep. This is when Elizabeth chose to strike.

Elizabeth put on the latex gloves, donned the gun her mother had given her, and stepped into her family home's hallway. She then slowly and quietly crept down the hall to her parent's bedroom. She entered, walked up to David, pointed the gun at his head, and fired. After a few seconds, Elizabeth noticed that David was making a gurgling noise, indicating that he was still breathing. To finish the job, Elizabeth then put the nozzle of the gun against her father's chest and fired again. David was silent.

After the second shot rung out, Joan, newly awake, told Elizabeth to get rid of the gun and go back to bed. Elizabeth obeyed. She brought the gun to her neighbor's house, which had been prearranged, and went back to her room. A few minutes later, she heard her mom call 911.

When the investigators arrived at the house, Elizabeth was calm. She had played her part in the plot and now couldn't do a thing besides sit back and watch her future develop beyond her control. Either the investigators would buy her mother's story and she would be fine, or investigators would discover their heinous plot and her life would be over.

Chapter 14: The Discovery

It didn't take investigators long to uncover the truth behind David's death. Joan openly admitted she was having an affair with Jeff, and when he was questioned, he had no problem telling investigators all about how Joan had wanted David dead. As it turned out, Joan's undying love for Jeff was unrequited. He did not feel as deeply for her as she did for him. He had no reason to protect her and was as candid as possible with police. He told them everything they needed to know to realize that Joan was ultimately the cause of David's death, whether she pulled the trigger or not.

On top of that, Elizabeth was not great at keeping secrets. She had told several of her friends about what happened on that night including Vera, who she had told in great detail not only about what she did that night but also how and why. The information Vera learned from Elizabeth was able to be corroborated by investigators, and it implicated not only Elizabeth, but largely Joan as well in David's murder.

On July 30, 2002, only eight days after David's murder, Joan Shannon was arrested and charged with first-degree murder. When police went to arrest Elizabeth for her role in the crime, she had mysteriously disappeared, but not for long. Police found, and promptly after arrested, Elizabeth on August 2. She had been hiding under a futon at a friend's house.

Once in custody, Elizabeth decided to try and salvage what she could of her life. She was honest with investigators and openly told them all about how her mother had emotionally manipulated and abused her into killing her stepfather. She was remorseful, she realized she had killed the only person who had shown any signs of actually caring about her. On August 15, Elizabeth pleaded guilty in court to Second Degree Murder and Conspiracy to Commit Second Degree Murder. In exchange for testimony against her mother, Elizabeth received the lenient sentence of 25-30 years in prison. She went into prison as a fifteen-year-old murderess and would not leave until she was in her 40's.

Joan, however, continued to be her selfish self. She continually denied any involvement in the murder plot and attempted to place all blame on her daughter Elizabeth. Investigators did not buy this story, and instead realized that pinning the murder on Elizabeth entirely had most likely been her plan from the outset.

Joan pleaded not guilty to all the charges laid against her including First Degree Murder and Conspiracy to Commit First Degree Murder and was found guilty after a grueling trial. She received a life sentence. In 2007, Joan attempted to file an appeal, which was promptly denied.

Joan will spend the rest of her life in prison.

Bonus story : CELESTE BEARD

"She is really in my mind, a really despicable human being." - crime writer Diane Fanning

Millionaire executive Steven Beard woke up screaming.

Experiencing excruciating pain, he reached down and clutched his stomach. He felt the blood on his hands and panicked. His internal organs were oozing outside his belly.

Beard reached over and called for an ambulance. The paramedics worked in vain to stem his bleeding. The seventy-four-year-old writhed in pain but out of the corner of his eye, he saw his wife Celeste enter the room.

"Oh my God," Celeste said. "Steve! What happened?"

The medics pushed the woman back, not wanting her to interfere in his care.

Chaos ensued as his thirty-seven-year-old wife and her two twin daughters entered the room. Police searched around the premise and found a shell on the ground.

Steven Beard had been shot in his stomach.

But by whom?

Was it the wife who strangely was not sleeping in the same bed. The daughters?

Or would it be Tracey Tarlton, a lesbian lover of Celeste?

"They knew Tracey had pulled the trigger," crime writer Diane Fanning said. "But they suspected someone else was involved. But Tracey just wouldn't talk."

Tarlton harbored a secret from the police. She had fallen in love with Beard's wife, Celeste.

But as Tracey would later find out, there was a lot about Celeste that she didn't know about...

CHAPTER ONE

"Celeste Beard had a very rough childhood," Fanning said. "There was a lot of instability, alcoholic abuse in the family and she really had it rough."

The identity of Beard's biological parents has remained a mystery. She was one of four children raised by adoptive parents, Edwin and Nancy Johnson. Celeste would claim that both Edwin and one of her older adoptive brothers would sexually abuse her from age 4 to 12. Nancy, her adoptive mother, was psychologically unstable and be institutionalized on a regular basis.

On one occasion, Celeste's daughter Kristina would record a conversation she had with Celeste in which she talked about her sexual abuse.

"Do you know what it feels like when you're four years old, you aren't even in kindergarten? Do you know what that does to you?"

Celeste has maintained that both adoptive parents physically abused her when she was a child and that she had tried to kill herself during her early teens. At the age of seventeen, she married Craig Bratcher and gave birth to twins, Jennifer, and Kristina. The relationship with Bratcher was a volatile one, filled with physical assaults and restraining orders. The couple would divorce and Beard would lose custody of the twin daughters.

But Celeste could get men to marry her with ease. Easy come, easy go.

She would go on to marry Henry Wolfe, an Air Force mechanic. Once again, the relationship was tempestuous and Celeste would divorce. She would claim later that her own divorce lawyer gave her money to have a boob job done.

She would then move to Arizona and marry a man named Jimmy Martinez. Celeste had a gutter mouth and would spew vulgarities without any kind of filter. She would refer to Martinez' penis as the "BMW" (Big Mexican wiener) but the two would get divorced despite the alleged size of her husband's package.

By the time Celeste reached her mid-thirties, she was desperate for a better life. She worked as a waitress at the Austin Country Club.

"To use an old-fashioned term," Fanning said. "Celeste Beard was a fortune hunter and she was determined to make her way in the world on the back of someone else."

She would meet the wealthy Steven Beard at the Country Club, fawning over the elderly man as he dined with his wife, Elise.

"At the time, Steven was married to Elise," Fanning said. "And from what everyone was saying, they had a wonderful and happy marriage. Then Elise died of cancer and when that happened Celeste knew what she wanted."

She wanted a rich man.

Steven Beard would do.

CHAPTER TWO

Steven Beard was a self-made millionaire. He served in the Navy and went to college at both TCU and SMU. He started his career in radio advertising in Dallas, literally starting at the bottom. By the 1970s, he had graduated to television and in 1981 he had become the general manager of KBVO in Austin, Texas. Four years later, the station would become one of the first affiliates of the now behemoth Fox Network. The station grew by leaps and bounds and Beard would sell his share in the company which completed his fortune.

Celeste targeted the newly widowed Steven for his money. She preyed upon the loneliness and loss of the TV executive and he fell for her charm.

"She paid attention to him," Steven's daughter Becky Beard said. "That's what she needed at the time. That's what he needed the most was for someone to pay attention to him. And he just went hook, line, and sinker."

Three weeks after his wife died, Steven would take Celeste out on a date.

He took Celeste to Mama Mia's Italian restaurant then they had a nightcap at his mansion. The executive then allowed Celeste to borrow his $50,000 Lexus and drive herself home.

Steven spared no expense in his courtship probably figuring that the he could make up for the age difference between the two of them with money. He courted the thirty-eight years younger woman with an open checkbook which included a $16,000 diamond cocktail ring, a $3,000 wristwatch, and a new SUV.

But Steven's family, specifically his daughter, grew suspicious of Celeste's interest in her father.

"I think it was money," Becky said. "I think Celeste was after his money."

"Celeste was in dire straits," Orange said. "She had nothing but bad luck in life and men but always failed to see her own hand in her circumstance. With Steven, she had an older man who would overlook all of those things. He would be able to use his money to bail Celeste out of her debt, depression and dumb choices."

Steven had enough money to give Celeste a clean slate. Celeste had committed insurance fraud during her time in Arizona with Jimmy Martinez and had a $20,000 restitution bill that Steven ultimately paid for.

He then funded a renewed custody battle for Celeste's twin daughters. She would win the case and become reunited with Jennifer and Kristina. The couple did not inform the teen daughters of their union until later. Celeste would pretend to be Steven's housekeeper until one of her daughters caught the two in a hotel room during the 1993 Super Bowl.

The union did not have the blessing of Steven's family. They all thought she was marrying him for his money. Steven ignored their counsel and decided to marry Celeste. He was smart enough to have a prenuptial agreement drawn out. In the agreement, Celeste would receive over half-million dollars if they divorced but she would receive up to six million upon his death.

CHAPTER THREE

Celeste took immediate advantage of her newly acquired status as Mrs. Steven Beard. She went on a shopping spree after shopping spree, wildly spending money on whatever whims she could dream up.

"She was insane about spending money," Fanning said. "She could have gone a year and a half wearing a different pair of shoes and purse every day and not run out. At one point he gave her one million outright and she went through it in record time, like six months."

A part of the marriage agreement that Celeste didn't like was the fact that she had to play the role of a loving wife. She had no problem putting on appearances anywhere outside the bedroom. But in the bedroom was where the problem lay.

Celeste didn't want to have sex with Steven.

"She married him only for money," Fanning said. "So obviously she didn't find a seventy-five-year-old man attractive. So she really didn't want to be sexually involved with him."

On February 18th, 1995, Steven and Celeste would exchange vows at the Austin Country Club. Their honeymoon night involved a "sex needle" wherein Celeste had to insert a syringe into the base of Steven's penis in order for it to stiffen. She described the practice as "unromantic" and "kind of traumatizing."

In the months that followed, Steven wanted more sex than Celeste could put up with as she would refuse to inject the syringe into his penis. Feeling gypped, Steven would file for divorce four months after the wedding but changed his mind after Celeste came up with the "oral sex solution".

Sunday mornings would be reserved for pleasing Steven sexually, a day she referred to as the "Sunday Suck."

Celeste would do her wifely duties with great reluctance. She told her daughters that there should be no distractions at all during her Sunday morning time with Steven. She wanted to get things over with as fast as she could.

Things were going well for Steven. He was happy to have a hot, younger wife performing sex for him once a week.

That is, he was happy with the happy endings until he started to feel the financial burn.

Steven had given Celeste a $10,000 a month allowance but she thought of that as mere chicken feed. She had three walk-in closets that she lined with hundreds of pair of shoes, each with a purse to match. She would go on $50,000 shopping sprees and lavish her friends with gifts and parties. The couple would also take lavish vacations, on one occasion they visited China for a month where they spent over $100,000.

Steven started his marriage with over twelve million dollars in net worth. After only a year of marriage to Celeste, he was down to a rapidly dwindling eleven million.

Celeste would want more.

Much more.

CHAPTER FOUR

Celeste pressed Steven for even more money. She argued daily that the half-million prenuptial agreement was too low. She pressed Steven for more money and he would not budge. But Celeste would not let the issue go until one day Steven just relented. He wrote Celeste a check for a half-million dollars.

Six months later, Celeste had blown through the money.

Then she wanted more.

At that point, Steven blew up. He threatened to cut off all of her credit cards.

"Celeste told Steven that she was going to kill herself if Steven cut off her money supply," Orange said. "Shopping was like a drug for her. She had to have her daily fix. Just going to a mall to buy a pair of cheap shoes wouldn't do it for her. She had to have it all. Every day."

And now Steven no longer wanted to pay the price.

"She had to buy things in order to feel good," Orange said. "It wouldn't have mattered how much she purchased. It would have never been enough. Nothing would ever have been enough."

The final straw was the Christmas holidays of 1998. Celeste had spent nearly $300,000 dollars over a few weeks. Steven went ballistic and the shit started to hit the fan. Celeste grew more contemptuous of Steven as he questioned her spending. She often referred to him as "the fat bastard" or "the old fool."

"What the hell is that old man still doing alive?" she would cry out.

Celeste would start to act out even more. She would leave the mansion for long stretches and spend time at a weekend home that Steven owned along the river. She would not go there alone as she often entertained her ex-husband, Jimmy Martinez.

Steven would eventually find about her extra-marital trysts and threaten divorce.

This prompted Celeste to threaten suicide as a form of retaliation. She would be sent to a psychiatric facility called St. David.

There she would meet a woman named Tracey Tarlton.

Tracey was a manager at a trendy bookstore called the BookPeople. She was also an unstable mental patient who was looking for a girlfriend. One look at the glamorous Celeste was all it took for Tracey. She had to try her hand at seducing the heterosexual and married woman.

"Tracey was an emotionally unstable woman who had been in and out of hospitals for depression and other disorders for quite some time," Fanning said.

The two hit it off.

Tracey would claim that Celeste was "extremely flirtatious" with her in the beginning. She said that the two first had sex on March 20th, 1999 and that their relationship would continue until the day she would shoot Steven.

The two were not discreet about their romance. A photo of a company get together showed Celeste sitting on her lesbian lover's lap. People at the party would later report seeing the women kissing passionately.

Celeste was not a lesbian but she was willing to engage in a relationship with Tracey in order to get what she wanted. She admitted during an interview with a psychiatrist that she had to drink copious amounts of alcohol in order to prepare herself for sex with Tracey. Her daughters began seeing books about lesbian love around the house.

But while Celeste had to numb herself with alcohol, Tracey needed no such aids.

She was immediately smitten by Celeste and wrote her love letters just weeks after they met.

"Celeste, you are so beautiful," Tracey wrote. "I think about your long, silky body and your incredible, long legs and I just can't stand it. And then I think of your incredible face and I want to...stand outside your building and wait until I get arrested. We won't even talk about what happens when I think about your sweet, tough, sexy voice."

"Celeste had no problem trading sex for favors," Orange said. "So she used her sexuality in order to get Tracey to do her bidding."

And that bidding would be murder.

CHAPTER FIVE

When Celeste returned home, she could no longer hide her contempt for her husband. She would drug his drinks and then sneak out of the home to party with Tracey.

She couldn't just divorce the millionaire, however, as she had signed a pre-nuptial agreement.

"Because Celeste had signed a pre-nuptial agreement," Fanning said. "She was only guaranteed a minimum amount of money if she divorced Steven and he'd already given her that money and she'd blown it."

Celeste's daughters would catch their mother in bed with Tracey on occasion. Steven, always a step behind, would find out about Tracey just like he found out about Martinez. He would catch them sharing a lesbian kiss on the lips and would promptly chase Tracey out of the house.

Tracey feared for the future of their relationship after it became out in the open. She was in love with Celeste and fantasized about sharing a life together.

Celeste knew this and decided to use Tracey as a pawn.

Going into her best drama queen act, she tearfully told Tracey about how Steven would verbally abuse her on a daily basis. His constant belittling would leave her feeling suicidal.

"What are we going to do?" Tracey asked.

"I don't know," Celeste said. "Maybe we could kill him?"

"We?"

The idle talk soon turned serious as Tracey would do anything to keep Celeste in her life. Both women sat down and began discussing various ways of murdering Steven.

Their first idea was using a homemade botulism technique. They set some food aside, allowing it to spoil and rot. The two women then ground up the presumably poisonous substance and sprinkled it on a chili dog that the served to Steven.

Both of them watched in eager anticipation as Steven placed tainted food into his mouth.

"Jesus," Steven said as he munched on the hot dog. "This is delicious!"

After that attempt didn't so much as produce a tummy ache, the two women spiked Steven's Vodka with 190-proof alcohol (everclear).

The old man passed out and then they fastened a plastic bag around his head. The bag did not have the effect they wanted as he breathed just fine as he slept off the alcohol.

Feeling desperate, they decide to sprinkle grounded up sleeping pills and ecstasy tablets over his steak.

"Wow," Steven said as he chewed on the tender steak. "This is delicious!"

Nothing worked and the two inept killers became more desperate.

Celeste went into her drama queen act again. She told Tracey that she was dreading an upcoming trip to Europe.

"He's going to make me sleep with him," Celeste said in tearful disgust. "I just can't take it. I can't take it anymore."

"I want to help," Tracey said.

"Then do something!"

"Like what?"

"Kill him," Celeste said. "Kill him for me"

CHAPTER SIX

Tracey was willing to do anything for her lover. Celeste came over to her place and Tracey showed off her 20-gauge shotgun. Her father had given it to her as a gift and had her name engraved on the bottom.

"We can use this," Tracey said as Celeste looked the gun over in fake admiration.

"Tracey was there to do the bidding of Celeste," Orange said. "Celeste had all of the power in the relationship."

"Celeste planned the killing out very carefully," Fanning said. "She drugged her husband's drink to make sure he fell asleep. She went into the other wing of the house where she could justifiably say she heard nothing. Then she left the doors open so that Tracey could sneak in."

Tracey was more than a willing accomplice. She believed that once Steve was eliminated, she and Celeste could finally be together.

On October 2nd, 1999 Tracey stepped into the bedroom of the Beard home and shot Steven in his stomach.

"I had stepped into a space that was just numb when I went into that bedroom," Tracey recalled. "And I shot him."

Steven looked over and saw that his guts were literally, outside his stomach.

"911, what's your emergency?"

"I need an ambulance," Steven said in a pained voice. "Hurry."

"What's the emergency?"

"My guts just jumped out of my stomach. They blew out. Yeah, they blew out of my stomach. They're lying on my stomach."

"OK, they're lying on your stomach?"

"Yes, I'm in bed. I'm in awful pain. I'm having a hard time figuring out what happened. I don't know what happened. I've never had this happen before."

Steven was shell-shocked. He had slept through the gunshot but awakened to find himself with a hole in his stomach.

Deputy Alan Howard was the first to arrive at the Beard estate. He rang the doorbell and banged on the front door but received no answer.

Heard headed around toward the side window and saw Steven writhing in pain on the bed. He busted through the sliding glass and entered.

Sgt. Gregory Truitt arrived as well and the two officers thought that Steven had a surgical incision of some sort ripped open.

Two women then entered the bedroom, Celeste, and her daughter Kristina. A few minutes later, a deputy found a shotgun shell near the bed.

The medical emergency now had become a designated crime scene.

Police searched the home and found the bathroom ransacked. But they realized that the drawers that were ransacked "looked too deliberate."

"This wasn't a burglary gone bad," one of the deputies said. "It was a murder attempt staged to look like a break-in."

CHAPTER SEVEN

Tracey had performed the shooting in the belief that Celeste would do her part. Part of her job was to remove any and all evidence that

Tracey was even there, one of which involved removing any shell casings.

But Celeste never picked up the shotgun shell.

She did keep quiet when the investigation ensued. Every family member and friend pointed to Tracey as a possible suspect except Celeste.

Police arrived at Tracey's home and asked if she had a gun. The woman agreed and the police requested that they test the rifle.

A ballistics match was made and Tracey would be arrested.

Steven would not die immediately from the gunshot wound.

His condition stabilized after seven surgeries. He would die four days after being released from the hospital as the wound become infected.

Celeste would remain by his side throughout his prolonged hospital stay.

But she also found time to shop, spending an astonishing $660,000 from October 1999 to March of 2000.

Steven would succumb from the wounds in January of 2000. Tracey Tarlton would be tried and convicted to life in prison for his murder.

True to her word, Tracey would remain silent in regards to Celeste's involvement.

But the police kept after her. They would try to reason with Tracey at first. When that didn't work, they would resort to taunting tactics.

"She really doesn't care about you," the police interrogator would say. "You're going to do the time for her crime?"

The police wouldn't let go because they knew Celeste was involved. But they needed Tracey's testimony.

"The first mistake Celeste made was that she wasn't in the same bed as Steven," Orange said. "When medics arrived, she came into the room and was clearly not sleeping with her husband. Surely that would raise a few eyebrows with police."

"They kept pressuring Tracey," Fanning said. "Trying to get her to give up Celeste because they knew there was no reason for Tracey to do this completely on her own."

Tracey would remain silent. She would wait in her jail cell for the visit from the love of her life, Celeste Beard.

But Celeste was not going anywhere near Tracey's cell.

She now had Steven's money. She didn't need anything else.

CHAPTER EIGHT

Celeste would eventually contact Tracey again. She would go into her drama queen act again, only this time the play acting would force Tracey's hand to break up with her.

Celeste then believed she had gotten away with everything scott free. Her lesbian lover had taken the fall for the murder. She now had carte blanche to Steven's estate, selling off one of the properties for a cool two million.

But like a curse that followed her around throughout her life, all of Celeste's ill-gotten gains would be short lived.

Celeste would marry Cole Johnson, a local bartender, and part-time musician she would meet in a bar in Aspen, Colorado.

Problem was that Tracey would find out about the union.

"Tracey became enraged when she read the marriage announcement," Orange said. "Here she was taking the fall for someone that she believed had loved her. Now this woman was off to a honeymoon in Aspen, Colorado. At that point, she had to realize that Steven was the victim and not her. She must have felt a sinking in her stomach at the realization that she was being played for so long."

Tracey informed the warden that she was ready to talk. She would tell the police the full story of what happened that night in Austin.

CHAPTER NINE

Nearly a year after orchestrating her husband's murder, Celeste Beard would be brought to trial and found guilty of first-degree murder.

"It was wonderful," Steven's daughter, Becky Beard said after Celeste's guilty verdict was announced. "It was absolutely wonderful. It was 'thank you, Lord.'"

"What brought Celeste down was greed," Fanning said. "Self-centeredness. And a willingness to do anything she wanted no matter who stood in the way."

"celeste had initially arrived at Steven's estate with one box of all of her possessions," Orange said. "Steven, in turn, gave her a lake house, a mansion, diamond jewelry, and allowed her to no longer have to work for a living. And how did she repay him? She killed his ass."

Steven Beard's family was allowed to address Celeste during sentencing. His son, Steven, told Celeste to go burn in hell.

But Celeste's own daughter turned on her.

"You say we turned on you," Kristina said. "Well, you turned on us. You turned on the whole Beard family. He let you into his home, loved you, honored, obeyed you, and you violated him and murdered him...Shame on you!"

Celeste will not be eligible for parole until the age of 80. She did not receive the six million "owed" to her after Steven's death. The proceeds of the Beard estate went toward his own children but also to Celeste's daughters, whom he had adopted.

Celeste continues to deny her involvement and now blames her incarceration on her daughters.

"They had two million reasons to lie," she said from her jail cell.

PSYCHO GIRL : THE TRUE STORY OF CATHERINE BIRNIE

123

JENA DICKENS

Catherine Margaret Harrison was born on May 23rd, 1951. Her partner, David John Birnie, was born on February 16th, 1951 and died on October 7th, 2015 by way of suicide. The duo was famously known throughout Australia as: The Killer Couple. They were from Perth, Australia and were found to have murdered four women ranging in age from 15 to 31 years old, over a span of about five weeks. Their fifth victim managed to escape through the bedroom window, while Catherine was distracted by a knock at the front door. The woman immediately ran and found help. The press referred to the heinous murders as the Moorhouse Murders. The victims were taken to Catherine and David's home located at 3 Moorhouse Street in Willagee, in Western Australia, a suburb of Perth.

Catherine was only two years old when her mother died in childbirth while giving birth to Catherine's younger brother. Her brother also died, two days later. Catherine's father, Harold, couldn't manage raising Catherine on his own at that time so she went to live with her maternal grandparents. When she was ten years old, Harold petitioned the court to receive custody of Catherine again, and he won. There always seemed to be a battle. Catherine's father didn't want her, but then wanted her, always back and forth. After Catherine was convicted of four counts of murder, it caused her father to suffer a nervous breakdown.

When Catherine was twelve years old she met a boy named David Birnie and they began dating two years later when they became teenagers. Both Catherine and David came from dysfunctional families. Their home life was chaotic and messy, literally as well as figuratively. David's mother was an alcoholic and his father was away at work the majority of the time. His father died in 1986 after battling a long illness. The house, as well as his mother, were messy and unkempt. She left her older children in charge of taking care of their younger siblings. She refused to do anything when it concerned the children and their welfare. Allegedly, David's mother would leave the refrigerator door open so that the children could eat throughout the day. David was the oldest of five children. David's school friends, as well as the local priest, deemed the family dysfunctional. The parents never prepared meals for their children, the house was always a mess, and the Priest, before marrying David's parents, said that he felt that their marriage would never lead to anything good. Little did he know how accurate his assumptions would be.

Catherine and David met through mutual friends shortly after David's family moved to the same Perth neighborhood as Catherine and her father. Catherine's father felt that David was trouble and a bad influence. Catherine had begun getting into a lot of trouble with the local police ever since the two of them met. Harold begged and pleaded with Catherine to stay away from David and stay out of trouble. Of course, this just brought the two closer. Whenever two kids are told not to do something, they go out of their way to blatantly disobey.

Even in adolescence David began exhibiting violent and perverse behavior. When David turned fifteen he dropped out of school and began working as jockey apprentice for Eric Parnham at the Ascot Race Course. While there, David would hurt the horses and also began his perverse career as an exhibitionist. David committed his first rape shortly after. By this point he had spent time in and out of jail for several charges ranging from misdemeanors to felonies. He built up a reputation around town as a sex and pornography addict.

Catherine was an accessory to a lot of crimes because of her involvement with David. They built up an extensive history of numerous charges including: breaking and entering, trespassing, unlawfully driving a motor vehicle, and theft. Catherine took the time, while in jail, to decide it was time to get away from David and start over. David had to serve a long jail sentence, while Catherine got off with probation. With the help of her parole officer, she found a job as a housekeeper working for the McLaughlin family. She ended up marrying the families' oldest son, Donald McLaughlin, on her twenty first birthday. They went on to have seven children. One of her children, however, was killed in a car accident while he was only an infant, leaving her with six of her children to take care of. Catherine was never really interested in motherhood though, and wasn't proud of her children and her family like another mother might be. She wasn't concerned about the children or keeping up with the house. Catherine was never truly happy. Her thoughts kept going back to her childhood love, David Birnie. The family that she had left never saw Catherine as a violent or evil person. Not unless she was around David.

Catherine finally reconnected with David Birnie after a thirteen year separation, four weeks after she gave birth to their seventh child. David had escaped from prison and the two of them had begun seeing each other. Catherine left her family and everything behind when David popped back into her life. They finally moved in together and Catherine had her last name changed to Birnie, although the couple never formally or legally got married. They moved into a white brick, two bedroom bungalow on Moorhouse Street. The house was unkempt, the property looked untended, and the house needed a fresh coat of paint. Catherine was completely dependent on

David, emotionally and physically. Catherine was easily controlled and manipulated by David, and she would do anything and everything to make him happy. She never wanted to disappoint him. David had an insatiable sexual appetite and was said to have sex up to six times a day. He also accrued an extensive pornography collection and his brother claimed he always had someone. He always had a woman around. David's brother, James, had ended up staying with Catherine and David for a short while. James had just recently been released from prison after serving time for his own sex related offenses. He stayed with the couple for about six months. His brother went on to describe the numbing spray that David would spray on his penis before he had sex with all of the different women.

David and Catherine had exhausted all of their options sexually and began looking for new ways to pleasure themselves. They had spoken about abduction and rape, but had not realized that it would be just a few short weeks before they turned their fantasies into a heinous and perverted reality. Being as emotionally dependent on David as she was, it was easy for David to talk her into his abduction and rape plans. Catherine could never tell him no. She felt that she couldn't survive without him and would do anything to keep him. Catherine was completely codependent and David always seemed to be in control. She wanted David to have all the pleasure and excitement that he wanted but knew that they had exhausted all efforts between just the two of them.

The abductions, rapes, and brutal murders began on October 6th, 1986. The couple didn't really care who their victims were, as long as they were female and alone. Twenty two year old Mary Neilson arrived at the Moorhouse Street residence to inquire about some tires that David had for sale. Mary was a student at the University of Western Australia where she was pursuing her degree in Psychology. Once inside the house, David took Mary by knife point and chained her to their bed and gagged her. Catherine stood in the room and watched as David raped the girl repeatedly. After the rape, the couple took Mary to Gleneagles National Park. David raped her one more time and then strangled her with a nylon cord and stabbed her through the heart. The couple then buried Mary in a shallow grave. Catherine looked on while David committed these violent acts, however, she did not yet participate.

The second murder took place on October 20th. The victim was fifteen year old, Susannah Candy. Susannah was a high school student attending Hollywood High School. She lived with her parents and had two brothers and one sister. Catherine and David Birnie had been driving around for several hours that night in search of their next victim. The couple finally found a girl walking along Stirling Highway, by herself, trying to hitch a ride. As soon as she got into David's car she had a knife to her throat and she was taken to the Birnies' home. While at the home, she was forced to write letters to her family explaining that she decided to run away. David repeatedly raped Susannah while she lay bound and gagged. Catherine had gotten into the bed with them and tried to strangle her with the nylon cord, but Susannah began fighting back. They forced sleeping pills down her throat, and once she passed out they successfully strangled her with the cord. The couple took Susannah to the State Park and buried her in a shallow grave, like their previous victims. This was the first time that Catherine took part in the murder. Catherine never showed any form of remorse over what she had done. When later asked why she contributed she said, "I wanted to see how strong I was within my inner self. I didn't feel a thing. It was like I expected. I was prepared to follow him to the end of the earth and do anything to see that his desires were satisfied. She was a female. Females hurt and destroy males."

On November 1st, the Killer Couple comes across their third victim, Noelene Patterson. Noelene was on her way home from work when her car ran out of gas. Noelene was a bar manager and had been working at Nedland's Golf Club that day. She was standing beside her car when David pulled up to her and offered his help. The thirty one year old got into David's car and was immediately met with a knife at her throat. She was taken to Moorhouse Street where she was bound and gagged, while being raped repeatedly. The original plan, like the others, was to kill the girl that same night. David had seemed to develop feelings for Noelene however. Catherine noticed the fondness that David had for the woman and became extremely jealous and increasingly upset. Noelene represented the type of person that Catherine could only wish to be and she absolutely despised her because of this. Catherine gave David an ultimatum at this point. She put the knife to her own chest and said, 'you either kill her tonight, or I will kill myself.' It was on the third night, after being given the ultimatum, that David gave Noelene several sleeping pills and then strangled her. She was then taken to the park and buried beside the other victims. Catherine admitted to taking pleasure in throwing sand in the victims face as David coldly buried her with no remorse.

Catherine and David's fourth victim, Denise Brown, suffered the same fate as the previous women who had the unfortunate experience of crossing paths with the Killer Couple. Denise Brown was twenty one years old, and was taken on November 5, 1986 while waiting at a bus stop. She was gagged and raped repeatedly before being put into the car and taken to Pine Plantation, where she was raped again while David waited for a blanket of darkness to fall. After it got dark he took her out and raped her again, while stabbing her in the neck. As David began burying her, thinking she was dead, Denise surprised the couple by sitting straight up in her grave. David struck her in the head twice with an axe as Catherine looked on in shock and amazement. David has said that he learned bodies would decompose at a faster rate if you stabbed them.

Detective Sergeant Paul Ferguson was the first to realize that he could be dealing with a serial killer, after the fourth woman was reported missing. Years later he recalled his experience while working on the case. He recalls how this case still haunts him and when asked why replied, "Because it was the most interesting and horrific I've had in my career," and "I have things tucked away back here that I pray to God I never pull out of the drawer." All of the missing women had come from relatively good homes and they never got into any real trouble. Their families found the phone calls and letters they received very suspicious.

The couples' fifth and final victim was seventeen year old Kate Moir. She was on her way home, after a night out with her friends, when she was abducted by the couple. The date of this final abduction was November 10th, 1986. Kate was the only one of their victims that was able to escape and run and find help. David had left the house for work that day. Catherine was home with Kate. She forced her to call her parents and tell them that she would be staying at a friend's house. When Catherine heard a knock at the door, she left Kate alone, untied, and went to see who was there. Kate took the opportunity to escape through the open window and ran half naked to the nearest store. She ran in crying and pleading for help. Kate was taken to the Palmyra police station and questioned. She was able to give the police a full description of Catherine and David, as well as inform the police of the couples' address. After their arrest, Catherine admitted to knowing Kate, but the couple said that the sexual acts were consensual and she was a willing participant. The police performed a search of the Birnie's home and found Kate's bag, as well as a pack of cigarettes that Kate had managed to hide in the ceiling in order to prove that she was there. After hours of questioning, Catherine and David finally admitted to the rape and murders of the four women and agreed to show the police where they had buried them. Three of the victims had been buried in Gleneagle State Forest and one on the Pine Plantation. The couple showed no emotion, whatsoever, as the police dug up the graves. David was the one who showed the police the locations of the women, except for one. Catherine insisted that she be the one to show them where Noelene was buried. She showed no regret, only anger. She spat on Noelene's grave and made her strong feelings of hate toward her very vocal to the detective. She explained to the police, in great detail, how much she despised Noelene Patterson. As they were leaving, David turned to Detective Katich and said chillingly, "What a pointless loss of young life." They showed absolutely no remorse for what they had done. This statement stuck with the detectives for years to follow. They couldn't believe how little the couple seemed to care or regret what they had been done. In some ways, however, they thought Catherine was relieved that it was finally over.

Catherine admitted to not caring about participating in the rapes and murders of the women, until they got to Denise Brown. "I think I must have come to a decision that sooner or later there had to be an end to the rampage. I had reached the stage when I didn't know what to do. I suppose I came to a decision that I was prepared to give her a chance." The brutal manner in which Denise was murdered seemed to hit Catherine hard. She witnessed David not only stab her repeatedly but strike her in the head with the axe. "Deep and dark in the back of my mind was yet another fear. I had a great fear that I would have to look at another killing like that of Denise Brown, the girl he murdered with the axe."

In response to Kate Moir's escape, due to Catherine's carelessness with her victim, she said, "I knew that it was a foregone conclusion that David would kill her, and probably do it that night. I was just fed up with the killings. I thought if something did not happen soon it would simply go on and on and never end."

Kate Moir survived the abduction and attacks of Australia's most infamous serial killers. Instead of remaining a victim, she chose to be a survivor. She also sought to seek reform for the way her government handled cases like hers.

"I want to see no parole for wilful murder. I want a reintroduction of wilful murder as a charge. I want truth in sentencing. I want no parole for sex offenders and child sex offenders. We have been softening our justice system for years."

Kate Moir is a married woman and mother of three children. She constantly fights for the changes and justice she deserves. The following are quotes that were made by Kate, again concerning Catherine's parole and the possibility of her release.

"I want the legacy that I leave to be that of a survivor and a hero, not a victim. But enough is enough."

"I want the Attorney General to change the law and stop reviewing Catherine Birnie's parole. She does not apply for it herself, it is automatically reviewed and every time it happens, it causes me incredible pain."

"Every time I hear that her parole is being reviewed, I relive the nightmare. It causes significant trauma because I relive it and it feels like it happened yesterday. My name was always protected because I was a minor at the time I was captured, but due to the internet, if anybody googles my name it is everywhere and linked to the Birnie killings."

The couple appeared in court on November 12th, 1986. This was just two days after their fifth victim had escaped and they were arrested. The court proceedings took place at Fremantle Magistrates Court. They both refused any kind of representation, no plea was entered, bail was refused, and they were remanded into custody. Catherine allegedly took photos and the couple also recorded video of their criminal acts. At trial, the police were in possession of the video evidence. On February 10, 1987 a crowd gathered outside of the courthouse. When they saw the couple being ushered in for trial they screamed and chanted, "Hang the Bastards!" The community was outraged over the news of the serial killings that took place and wanted David and Catherine to receive the maximum sentence. They even wanted to reinstate the death penalty for David and Catherine Birnie.

Bill Power, the court reporter, spoke about the proceedings and the manners in which the couple acted while in court. He said that it would be something that would always stick with him, he would never forget.

"There was nothing distinctive about David and Catherine when they first appeared in court to face multiple murder charges in the serial

killings which brought an end to the mystery of young women going missing off Perth streets."

"They were a rather nondescript, ordinary looking couple you might find running a petrol station in a country town. David was a weedy little man and Catherine his drab, slightly buxom wife with a very sour face. Both were accompanied by male police officers."

"If you have ever witnessed a wild cat go off, then try and imagine some hellcat in the confined spaces of a narrow staircase. Catherine Birnie fought against the guarding police officers and refused to allow any of them to touch her as she screamed and spat her words at them until she reached the dock and spotted her beloved, David. Only then did she calm down."

It had also been said previously, by some people in the community that the couple never looked like the type that could commit such violent acts. They looked like normal and ordinary people. But the secret horrors of what occurred in their home on Moorhouse Street would paint a very different image of the couple.

Trial Judge Justice Wallace said in trial, "Each of these horrible crimes were premeditated, planned, and carried out cruelly and relentlessly over a comparatively short period."

Right before Judge Wallace sentenced Catherine, he delivered the following message to her. He explained that he did not believe that even though she pled guilty, that she was truly sorry for what she had done. She had pled guilty and avoided a long trial, and spared the victims' families from having to relive over and over what happened to their loved ones, but she showed no remorse, no emotion, no sympathy for the crimes she had committed with David Birnie.

"You willingly joined in the selection of your unfortunate victims, carried them off at

knifepoint, and held them in captivity for the sole purpose of the sexual gratification of your partner in crime and then murdered them, lest you be identified, and then finally mutilated them. You personally extinguished the life of two of your victims and certainly participated in the death of the third. The only appropriate punishment is the sentence I intend to impose, strict life security in prison."

Remember, Catherine was completely devoted, obsessed, and brainwashed when it came to David. She would do anything and everything for him to make sure he was happy. This is the driving factor that David used to manipulate and control her. He needed an accomplice and she was more than willing, and he knew it. Catherine and David received four separate life sentences for the abduction, torture, rape, and murder of Mary Neilson, Susannah Candy, Noelene Patterson, and Denise Brown. Under sentencing laws, their case was brought up every three years automatically for parole. Kate began a crusade to ensure that the couple remained in prison. She grew a social media presence and page entitled, We Support Kate, as well as worked with the Empowerment Foundation in an attempt to build an online reform petition. Kate also received support from Catherine's son, Peter. He chose not to release his surname to the public, due to the physical and emotional abuse he has been forced to face in relation to his mother's crimes. He had suffered personal and professional ruin, as soon as people learned about his family history. He had been turned down for jobs, lost jobs he had, and even lost his fiancé because of his family background. Peter was only five years old when his mother was arrested. He saw his mother on television because of it shortly after her arrest. When speaking out on the abuse he faced, he recalled horrible stories of what happened to him, and his siblings, while growing up. He also stated that the mandatory parole hearings, every three years, prevented him from getting on with his life. Having to hear about his mother and relive the violence his mother was responsible for every few years, was an interruption to his life, and it made it harder to maintain a sense of normalcy within his career life and personal life. In an interview with the West Australian, Peter stated, "I want the parole board to hear I don't want her out. I don't want to see her out." He also said, "I have had baseball bats to the head, I have been jumped on and kicked at. I have been knocked out."

After pleading guilty and receiving their sentences, David was initially sent to maximum security Fremantle Prison, he was eventually moved into solitary confinement. He did not get along with the other prisoners and was constantly getting into fights. The inmates frequently and violently attacked David. A day before he was due in trial for the charge of rape of an inmate, David hung himself in his jail cell. His suicide occurred in 2009 at Casuarina Prison. Catherine's request to attend David's funeral was refused.

Catherine was sent to Bandyup Women's prison where she was eventually employed as the head librarian. While in prison, the couple exchanged over 2600 letters, but were denied any other form of contact. Catherine's mandatory parole hearings were finally revoked in 2009, and her papers were subsequently marked: 'never to be released.'

While many people are against Catherine Birnie ever getting parole, one man stands against this argument. Perth QC Tom Percy disagrees with the opinion of people that had been saying that some people just don't deserve a second chance. The following quotes by Percy outline his argument of Catherine not remaining in prison and the likelihood of her harming the community, as well as his stance of being in favor of Catherine's parole.

"She should not be kept in prison to satisfy society's thirst for revenge."

"She has been there thirty odd years and you would think it might be time for us to say she has done her time. She has done her statutory minimum prescribed by the court, which was in possession of all of the facts."

"I am not sure she could really be a threat to anyone anymore, and all my information from Bandyup Womens' Prison is that she is a little old granny that goes about her work in the library like a church mouse."

"This case just so happened to be one that caught the public attention, even though she was not the prime mover in it. David is now dead."

"What's the point of keeping her in there? Sadly, it looks like she will never get parole, but I think she probably deserves it."

Despite his argument and fight to get Catherine released from prison, she still remains behind bars. She has not requested any new parole hearings, herself, as of yet. Some people in the community had gone as far as to say that if she were to be released, then maybe Percy should allow her to live with him in his residence.

It was now January of 1987. A letter written by Catherine Birnie, while in prison, eventually surfaced. It was a letter she had written to her six children in an attempt to explain some of her actions that led to her being placed in prison and why she left them in the first place. The letter reads as followed:

"Dear kids, Hi! Mum here...the reason I changed my name to Birnie was so that you kids wouldn't be hurt by the newspapers and television people. I am not proud of what has been said about me, but I have to live with that and the memories. As to why this happened, I can only

hope that the doctors can help me to find out.....I never stopped loving any of you kids. Maybe I was wrong about leaving you but I thought you would be safer with your father."

Catherine's husband, Donald, claimed that he had still wanted her back. This was after trial and after he heard of the horrific acts she had committed with David. He stated, 'you can't stop loving someone after fifteen years of marriage.' Donald's mother stood firmly beside her son, saying that Catherine had been good and non-violent, until David cast his spell over her. Catherine's nephew, Leonard Nock, stood beside his aunt claiming, "All Aunt Cathy wanted was someone to lean on. She never had a mother. She is a very caring person. She and I are very close. I used to call her my mum. She was never the violent type, she never used to hit the kids. It is not the Cathy we used to know and love." In Catherine's letter she also persuaded the children to tell their father to divorce her. She said their father needed to move on and this was the way it needed to be done. She didn't hold out any hope for her eventual release and didn't want Donald to wait for her, because it was never going to happen. She also asked the children to get permission from Donald to write back to her, and maybe even one day go and visit her. The family put the entirety of the blame on David. They refused to admit to or believe that Catherine had anything to do with the violence. During their prison visits, the family also failed to even ask Catherine the question regarding her guilt or innocence. They didn't want to hear the answer, therefore, they never even asked the question.

Catherine Bernie was up for parole in 2013 and again in 2016. She was denied both years. She is once again up for review sometime in 2019. "Now barring any reason to keep her in, and revenge I don't consider enough of a reason. She should be released."-Percy

Despite Percy's statements, Catherine Birnie remains in prison to this very day, with little to no chance of parole. People, even to this day, wonder if the abductions, the perverse rape, and heinous murders would have continued long past the few weeks they had gotten away with it. If they had never been caught, would they have continued? Finally, were there other victims that they never confessed to? Other gravesites that have yet to be located? It is too late for David Birnie to tell anyone, but Catherine still has the chance to admit to any other wrongdoing she had done before her permanent home in prison forced her to keep distance between herself and her lover. I guess we will never know.

"I honestly believe that woman has never given those victims one ounce of consideration, both the dead victims and the families of the

victims...They [David and Catherine Birnie] were parasites who lived off of each other. The most evil people I have ever, ever come across."-Detective Paul Ferguson.